PERFECT
CONTROL

PERFECT
CONTROL

A Driver's
STEP-BY-STEP GUIDE
to Advanced
CAR CONTROL
Through the
PHYSICS OF RACING

The Science of Speed Series

created by PARADIGM SHIFT DRIVER DEVELOPMENT
written by ADAM BROUILLARD

www.paradigmshiftracing.com

ISBN-13: 978-0997382402
ISBN-10: 0997382406

Published by Paradigm Shift Motorsport Books
Perfect Control and The Science of Speed Series are
trademarks of Paradigm Shift Driver Development.

www.paradigmshiftracing.com

For information about custom editions, special
sales, premium and corporate purchases please
contact:

Paradigm Shift Driver Development
development@paradigmshiftracing.com
470.240.1582.

CONTENTS

"It ain't what you don't know that gets you into trouble.
It's what you know for sure that just ain't so."
- Mark Twain

THE **LIMITS** OF **CONTROL**

When a novice first tries high-performance driving, they will often drive the same way on a racetrack that they do in every-day driving, only faster. This causes all kinds of issues when they get to the limit, because the car control cues and driver inputs they are used to completely change. This can be a problem, because if your goal is ultimate speed, the limit is where you need to be.

> Before you can fully utilize Line Theory rules, you must get to an almost automatic level of car control.

Let's imagine you need to pull into a parking spot at your local store. As you drive down the row, you eye your spot and then maneuver your car to the far side so you can get a wider entry. As you approach, you begin turning the wheel and maybe using a little brakes or throttle to change your speed, all the while focusing on the spot and predicting the path you need to take to arrive there correctly. You may make small alterations in your steering or other driver inputs to keep you on the ideal path into your spot. A key point here is that you most likely aren't even thinking about the steering, throttle, or brakes. All your attention is on the parking spot and the path you need to take to get there. The car control needed is basically automatic.

But what would the average driver do if turning the steering wheel sometimes made the car steer more and sometimes didn't? What if the car suddenly starting turning faster even if you didn't turn the steering wheel more? What if the brakes sometimes slowed you down and sometimes didn't, or the throttle seemed to sometimes just make you spin in place? Basically, everything the driver thought they knew about how the car should react seemed to change randomly. They would probably start walking to the store.

But these are exactly the types of responses a racing driver will have to learn to contend with and many become so overwhelmed that the majority of their attention shifts to controlling the car and not on where they need to go. Their car control is no longer automatic like that average driver in the parking lot.

Introduced in our book *The Perfect Corner*, Line Theory is the term we use for the physics-based set of rules a driver can use to optimize their line. While drivers of any skill level can begin to apply Line Theory rules, to fully exploit them, you must reach an almost automatic level of car control. To achieve this, you will first need to learn the correct cues and driver inputs needed to control a car at the limit. The car control cues would be all the information you are getting from the car and your surroundings. Primarily visual, auditory, and tactile. Driver inputs are your controls over the vehicle. Primarily brakes, throttle, and steering. How to gather the correct information from the cues and use it to optimize your driver inputs is the very essence of car control.

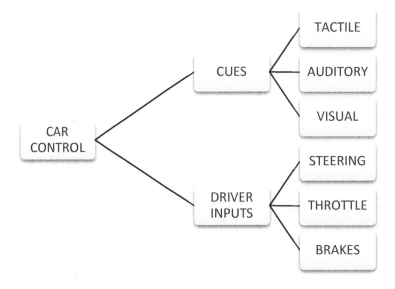

A **TIGHTROPE** ACT

Can you walk a tightrope? The vast majority of people would probably answer no. We know it is possible, because we have all seen it done, but what if you lived in a world where no one had ever done it and someone asked you to try. You would probably think it impossible and a quick try would reaffirm that thought.

So how does this relate to motor racing? While a tightrope is basically pass/fail, as you either fall off or stay on, driving a car is only as hard as a driver makes it. But to the average viewer, sometimes the difference is almost imperceptible. Watch a pretty fast local driver and to the untrained eye, they look like they are doing virtually the same thing as a world-class driver. Even an average racer in a relatively easy-to-drive car could probably get within a second or two of a world-class driver given specific instructions and a few weeks of practice. Only the stopwatch tells the ultimate difference, and the average racer most likely doesn't even know why they are slower. They might just chalk it up to having less talent or think maybe the world-class driver has figured out some sort of better line.

Pushing yourself to where you need to be might feel impossible at first, just like tightrope walking. But with practice, the impossible will become hard, and then manageable, and then eventually, second nature.

In reality though, the world-class driver is doing something just as hard as what a tightrope walker does and it takes more than a few weeks to learn this. To an average racer, what the world-class driver is doing would feel almost impossible. Just like a tightrope walker, they make a finally tuned balancing act at the limit of control look easy.

What this average racer doesn't realize is that they have essentially been walking around on a 6-inch wide board as they drive. They might every once in a while step up on the tightrope and fall off and then remind themselves to stay on the board, but unfortunately, walking around on a board will teach you very little about tightrope walking.

The first step to reaching a world-class level of car control is to realize you'll need to step onto that tightrope before you can start learning how to balance on it. This book will give you the tools needed to do that, but understand this is hard, very hard. It will take years to master. There is a reason most world-class drivers started as children. Pushing yourself to where you need to be might feel impossible at first, just like tightrope walking. But with practice, the impossible will become hard, and then manageable, and then eventually, second nature.

Is this car at the limit and oversteering or understeering?

To find out, a driver must test - change a driver input and check the car's response.

THE **LIMIT** DEFINED

So what is the limit? Ask 10 drivers and you might get 10 different answers. We define the limit as when no change in driver input can cause an increase in force. This sounds a little technical, but a simple example would be a driver traveling at a constant speed and then slowly tightening the steering. There would be a certain point where turning the steering wheel more would not make the car turn any tighter. The tires have reached their limit. In this example, it would be the front tires that reached their limit and many drivers understand this is called understeer. If the rear tires are what is limiting how much a car can turn, then you have oversteer.

For ultimate speed, you will always either be understeering and/or oversteering the entire way through a corner.

The key takeaway here is that anytime you are at the limit, you will either be understeering or oversteering. This also means that for ultimate speed, you will always either be understeering and/or oversteering the entire way through a corner. While theoretically it's ideal to use all four tires equally, it's not technically possible to be perfectly neutral and keep both front and rear tires at the limit at the same time. This would be a transient state at best, and as you'll see, it's actually impossible to know if you truly are at the limit of both at the same time. If you ever think you have achieved perfect neutral balance, it just means you haven't developed the sensitivity yet to detect whether you are actually understeering or oversteering.

CHANGE IS REQUIRED **(TESTING)**

So if we know we want to always be at the limit of understeer or oversteer in a corner, how can we ensure we are actually accomplishing that? Imagine you are driving through a corner and you think you are probably at the limit of understeer. How can you be sure? What cues do we have to guide us? It turns out the answer is actually quite simple, although often not very intuitive.

> The only way to know if you are at the limit is to change your driver input and check the vehicle's response. We call this process testing.

The only way to truly know if you are at the limit is to change a driver input and see what happens. Try turning the steering wheel more. Did the car tighten its turn? Then you weren't at the limit. Did the car not turn any faster? Then you were either at the limit or over it, possibly way over it. Being over the limit is typically bad, but the only way to find out how far over the limit you are is to unwind the steering until the car lessens its rate of turning a little. You have to make a change and see what happens.

We're actually getting a little ahead of ourselves here, as we aren't quite ready to get into the specific cues and driver inputs yet. But we did want to bring up this example to point out that the only way to know if you are truly at the limit or not is to change a driver input and see what happens. We call this process **testing**. To drive at the limit, you have to constantly be testing to see if you can generate any more force from the tires. This is why you often see top drivers making constant, small motions with the steering wheel during a corner. Testing can also be done with the throttle or brakes as well though.

During corner exit for example, you can test for the limit with the steering wheel or throttle, or a little of both. Ayrton Senna was known for testing the limit more with the throttle and less with steering. Some drivers will use the steering wheel more. Ideally, you will be trying to find the limit with both at the same time by making small modulations and checking the car's reaction. Understand though, that this is not going to be "Hmm, let me test now." It must be trained to the point that it is automatic and the driver will naturally try to stay at the limit by modulating their inputs. The more sensitive a driver is, the smaller these inputs can be, but they must always be there if the driver wants to **know** they are at the limit and getting the most out of the car.

The reason this is the only way to know for sure is that tire grip is an ever-changing target. No cue exists that can accurately tell you if you are currently at the exact peak of grip. The only way to know is to change an input and see if this increased or decreased the force acting on the car. Even a highly accurate tire-testing machine that was programmed to keep a tire as close to the peak of grip as possible would need at least some movement back and forth across the peak to do this. We'll talk much more about this as we continue, but just remember, if you aren't making some sort of driver input change and checking how the car reacts, you can't really know for sure if you are at the limit.

Ayrton Senna was known for a unique throttle stabbing technique to test for the limit.

PREDICTIVE VS REACTIVE DRIVING

A big difference between a driver and a basic tire-testing machine however, is that a driver has a memory and can learn. A driver will be able to adapt to a car and circuit and start predicting how much grip the car has in different situations. They will always have to test this limit with changes in driver inputs, but their predictions will allow them to stay closer to that grip peak more easily.

We call this need for constant testing **reactive** driving, and the learned adaptations a driver makes to a certain car and track we call **predictive** driving. When a driver does a practice session and their lap times are better at the end, that is an improvement in their predictive driving. The steady improvement in a driver's skills over the years if they train properly is an improvement in their reactive driving. Reactive driving represents a driver's core car control abilities.

> We call this need for constant testing reactive driving, and the adaptations a driver makes to a certain car and track we call predictive driving.

Unfortunately, many drivers don't recognize the difference and think the only way to get better is by simply improving their predictive driving. Doing countless laps in a certain car/track combo and learning every nuance of the circuit and car. We've found this can actually hinder one's ability to improve, as you are not pushing your core car control abilities to the limit and can end up driving too much by memory. Only focusing on improving predictions will cause a driver to lose a lot of time if they switch cars and it takes them a long time to learn new tracks. Although they can sometimes get to the front of the field with enough practice, they will rarely reach their ultimate potential.

On the other hand, the fastest drivers are the ones with amazing reactive driving abilities. In other words, they have great car control. They can adapt quickly to different tracks and cars. They are great in the wet because of their ability to control the car in a new situation quickly. But also importantly, if you have great reactive driving ability, you will be able to improve your predictive driving much faster and get up to speed on a new track or in a new car much quicker. Your practice time will be much more efficiently used. Some drivers think you are either born with this talent or not, but the good news is that reactive driving is something you can learn to improve. While there is certainly a genetic component that will allow some drivers to improve car control faster than others, most drivers are probably far from their ultimate potential because many don't know the proper cues and driver inputs to focus on and train.

Imagine you've started a team in the brand new World Championships of Braking. It's a competition to see who can stop a car from 100 mph in the shortest distance. This sounds like a silly competition, but we're using braking because it's relatively simple to understand the cues and driver inputs involved. On your team, you have two drivers starting with equal skill. They will train the exact same amount of time each day, but the first driver gets to always use the competition car, and the second driver must change cars every single time they practice and never gets to practice in the competition car except for a few minutes before their competition run. The first event is in a week.

Because braking is relatively straightforward, the first driver will probably get within a few feet of what would be optimum within a few days at most. Most likely, they would probably initially listen for tire squealing and start predicting how hard they need to push the brake pedal to reduce their stopping distance. There would be some trial and error where they try different pedal pressures and then check their distance. Eventually they would settle on a good solution where they have basically memorized how hard to push the pedal and their braking distance is usually within a few feet of optimal.

The second driver however, is being forced to use a different car every time and so this trial and error doesn't work. They are unable to improve their predictive driving and can only work on their reactive driving. They try basing their braking on listening for tire squealing, which is working okay, but they get pretty big variations in their stopping distance.

The first competition arrives and the first driver handily defeats the second driver, but is beaten by a few former F1 drivers who have gotten to practice in the competition car all week. This trend continues into the season with the first driver not really improving and always being beaten by the F1 drivers, but always beating the second driver. The first driver is happy with their results and thinks the F1 drivers are just more naturally talented.

Tired of always losing, the second driver has started to do some research because the tire squealing thing isn't really giving them very consistent performance. They need a more precise cue and so they start to pay attention to how fast they decelerate with different pedal pressures. This is primarily with their eyes, but also feeling the g-forces. Initially it's pretty frustrating and they feel like giving up, but they push through and with lots of work, they slowly start to improve their reactive driving ability based on this more precise cue. Introduced in *The Perfect Corner*, the second driver is now training himself to react to the Universal Cue. We'll talk much more about this later in the book.

The first season ends with the second driver finally running almost neck and neck with the first driver and the F1 drivers are now getting so good with the car that first and second is now often mere inches apart. The competition promoters feel like it's getting boring though and want to shake things up, so they've announced that for the next season the competition car won't be revealed until right before the event and everyone only gets a few minutes of practice.

On the day of the next season's first event, the first driver does their run and almost spins out, coming in near the bottom of the results. They just blame it on the car not fitting their driving style and maybe next time the car will be a better match for them. But the second driver feels totally at home, as they have been constantly driving new cars for over a year now. They come in third right behind the F1 drivers, and the top three are all within a few feet of each other. There is a much bigger spread in the overall results and it's clear which drivers have great reactive driving abilities and which don't. Given a few weeks of practice with the new car, the F1 drivers and now the second driver would probably all be within a few inches of each other again. The first driver just doesn't understand where the second driver's sudden talent came from.

> The better your reactive driving skills are, the faster you will be able to get up to speed and your practice time will be more efficiently used.

Hopefully this little story gave you a good idea of the difference between predictive and reactive driving. Of course, learning all the skills needed to drive a car on a road course is a good bit harder than just braking. It would certainly take longer than a year to compete with F1 drivers, but the principles are the same. Also, don't think we are saying that predictive driving is not important and you should not practice a car/track combo. If you have a race coming up soon, you'll want to spend the majority of your practice time on that. The better your reactive driving skills are though, the faster you will be able to get up to speed and your practice time will be more efficiently used.

UNIVERSAL **CONTROL**

In this last story, what would happen if the surprise car in the beginning of the second season had no normal brakes and only the handbrake worked? The second driver's reactive training wouldn't transfer nearly as well would it? The driver input needed would now be completely different to what they had trained and the tight connection they had developed between the Universal Cue and their braking foot would be useless.

While that would certainly be a problem, the good news is that the vast majority of cars have essentially the exact same control systems and improving your reactive driving ability will allow you drive them all more effectively. There are a few exceptions, but for the most part, we are talking about a rear-wheel drive car with a steering wheel, throttle, and brake pedal. Even common variations such as front-wheel drive, 4-wheel drive, and rear-brake only karts change things very little and you can basically use the same techniques on all of them.

So if that's the case, then why do you sometimes hear how you need to drive a certain car a certain way, you shouldn't trail brake that car, etc...? Basically, that different cars require different driving techniques. The reason is that some people make the same mistake that the first driver in our last story was making. They only learn to drive a car predictively, so when they switch to cars that require a different pedal pressure, optimal line, steering ratio, etc... all their memorized inputs don't work. Just like our first driver, many do this because they don't realize there is an alternative that allows them to improve their abilities in practically any vehicle. They never learn what they should ideally focus on and train. Although focusing on improving your reactive driving can initially be more difficult, the rewards are much greater as you will be improving your core driving ability. You will be able to adapt to virtually any car and track very quickly. You not only lower your potential best lap time, but also make much better use of your practice time.

PART 1 - CAR CONTROL CUES

A cue can be anything that gives you information about what the car is doing. These are not only things within the car; they can be external things such as where it currently is on track as well as the direction and speed it's moving.

The first part of the car control equation is the cues. A cue can be anything that gives you information about what the car is doing. These are not only things within the car; they can be external things such as where it currently is on track as well as the direction and speed it's moving. There are so many different things a driver can pay attention to that it's no wonder many can feel confused from hearing so many different pieces of advice from so many sources.

Another problem is that the best cues, although we'll see how they are actually quite simple, may not be very intuitive. Drivers that get into motorsport as adults often have the biggest problems. A more grown up, analytical mindset can often lead you off on tangents whereas the actual answer was in front of you the whole time. Naturally talented children that start racing early can have an easier time, as they tend to be less analytical and just try to "go fast," which as we'll see is actually just a simplified way of explaining the Universal Cue. By the time they are older and become more analytical, they already have this ability so well trained and ingrained in their reflexes that they often can't really articulate what they are doing. Not everyone is fortunate enough to start young though, so we'll work through this the other way around to achieve what a gifted child might do naturally.

VISUAL/G-FORCES

STEERING FORCES

TIRE NOISE

The Hierarchy of Cues

ANY **CUE** WORKS... TO A DEGREE

It's important to understand that while we are going to cover the very best cues to use, basically anything can work as a car control cue. You could put a cup of hot coffee in your lap and just drive faster until you start burning yourself. That would be a car control cue, not a very good one, but it's a cue. While not many people are driving based on a coffee burn cue, unfortunately the most commonly used cues are not necessarily based on how accurate they are, but on how easy they are to pick up on. It's easy to see why some drivers focus on things like tire noises and steering wheel forces. These are easy concepts to understand and although they can give you pretty good information in certain circumstances, they are ultimately imprecise cues, as we'll discuss shortly.

Even worse though, some drivers will use what we call arbitrary cues. A beginning driver might just drive based on fear of the unknown. They will simply drive to whatever they arbitrarily feel is "fast" because they are afraid the car will spin or do something unexpected if they go faster. But even a more experienced driver might use an arbitrary cue such as driving based on a percentage of what they feel is pushing too hard. They might drive at what they feel is 95% because when they drove at what they consider 100%, their lap times were slower. These numbers are only based on a subjective feeling though, so they are still arbitrary cues.

In the world of sim racing, some drivers try to incorporate cues that unrealistically alter the view or sound. They might also focus on imprecise cues like tire noise. They feel that because they lose the "seat of the pants" feeling that they need to compensate for this. The good news is that none of this is necessary. The best and most precise cues that work in real life will also work in sim racing although it can sometimes be harder to recognize them.

CUE PRECISION

There are many different cues that a car can provide and drivers are all trying to assimilate and combine these as best they can. But what happens when the driver gets conflicting information from different cues? This is often not something a driver might even realize is happening, but this conflict causes an inability to precisely control the car. An example of this would be if a driver were accustomed to steering more until the tires start squealing, but as the driver started to develop their other cues, they notice the car will sometimes still turn more even once the tires have started making noise. How do they know which to pay attention to?

> While a large number of cues can be used to get a driver close to the limit, very few can provide the precise information needed to tell you exactly what a car is doing. We call these precise cues primary cues.

This brings us to the concept of cue precision. While a large number of cues can be used to get a driver close to the limit, very few can provide the precise information needed to tell you **exactly** what a car is doing. We call these precise cues primary cues. The less precise cues we call secondary cues. Secondary cues might provide hints about what the car is doing and can be useful as a driver improves their recognition of the primary cues, but they will slowly become less important and eventually almost all together ignored as your skills improve.

As we go through the different cues, we will explain how each cue fits within these categories based on how precise of information they provide.

AUDITORY CUES – TIRE NOISE

Often the main cue used by many sim racers and beginning track enthusiasts, it's easy to see why some people tend to focus on tire noises. With many tires, especially street-based ones with tread blocks, you will often hear a squeal as you begin to approach the limit. The squealing noise is the sound of the rubber vibrating rapidly. With a street-based tire in the dry, if you aren't hearing any noise from the tire, it means you are most likely pretty far from the limit. Racing sims will often simulate these street tire sounds even on cars that are using racing slicks whereas in reality most racing slicks usually only start making a sound once past the limit. Some sim drivers will turn up these tire sounds and try to use them to gauge their grip levels.

So does this work? Yes, but again only to a certain degree. While some tires will start making noise as you approach the limit, there is no certain noise they make right at the peak of grip, so it is not a very precise cue. Remember, there is no cue that can accurately tell you if you are currently at the peak of grip. Only testing will tell you. It can also be hard to tell which tire or tires are making the noise and tire noises also tell you nothing about the very important information of which direction tire forces are going.

Therefore, tire noises are an imprecise secondary cue. They can be a pretty good crutch for a beginning driver who is just coming to terms with the concept of driving at the limit, but listening for tire noises should be discarded as early as possible as better cues take over. The one situation where you might want to hang on to this cue a little longer is for straight-line threshold braking. This is often one of the hardest areas for people to develop using the Universal Cue and listening for a tire squeal as a backup can save you from flatspotting tires.

AUDITORY CUES – ENGINE NOISE

Cues

The other major auditory cue is going to be listening to the engine speed. This certainly has its place for helping with shift points, but can also be used for other less obvious purposes as well. For instance, in a rear-wheel drive car during braking, a rear tire lockup can be heard as a quick drop in engine rpm. You probably wouldn't use this as a main cue while braking, but it might be useful when trying to set brake bias and it's important to understand why you might hear that sudden engine speed drop during a braking zone.

Excess throttle and wheelspin may or may not cause oversteer depending on a car's differential and setup.

You might also use engine noise as a cue during the corner exit phase to detect excessive wheelspin, as you will hear an unusually sharp rise in engine speed. This is only an imprecise secondary cue as there is no way to know the exact amount of wheelspin you need for maximum acceleration, but it is a good backup to know you went too far. This cue can be especially useful for open differential cars that have a tendency to spin up the inside rear. Detecting just the loss of acceleration from only inside rear wheelspin can be a good bit harder than noticing the oversteer that is typically associated with excessive wheelspin of both rear tires. So while engine noise is a precise cue in terms of telling you exactly how fast the engine is going, from a handling standpoint, it is still always going to be an imprecise secondary cue only used as a backup to more precise cues.

TACTILE CUES - STEERING FORCES

Tactile cues would be anything felt by the driver. This could be g-forces, steering wheel forces and position, and even feeling the position of the pedals. This category is often seen as very important by many drivers, but as we'll see, it's not nearly as important as some think and the best cues to focus on in here are also not immediately obvious.

Along with tire noises, steering forces are one of the first cues some drivers tend to focus on. This has reached almost mythical status in car culture with car companies pushing the great steering feel their cars provide. But while being able to feel every bump on the road might feel good from a subjective standpoint, once you start to understand the physics of car control, you'll discover that steering wheel forces aren't very useful for finding maximum grip. They can even be a hindrance sometimes. It also turns out the information you do get from the steering wheel that is useful might not be what you are expecting.

As a quick example of how steering forces are not a primary car control cue for finding maximum grip, consider racing karts. Because of their basic design, they have huge amounts of caster and scrub radius along with a very quick steering ratio. We'll cover these features in a minute and explain the specifics, but because of them, kart racers must deal with very heavy and quick steering, huge turning forces from bumps, and virtually no telltale steering force drop-off as a tire approaches the limit. Even with these limitations, great kart racers are still able to drive the kart at the limit and find the maximum grip available. If this information doesn't come from the steering wheel, how do they do this?

Kart racers must learn to sense the limit with more precise visual and g-force based cues as the steering wheel provides no real useful information about maximum grip. This is a great training tool, as when they make the move to cars, kart racers are already tuned into other, more precise cues.

Sim racers are another great example of drivers not needing steering wheel forces to drive at the limit. Most of the top sim drivers are equally good with all force feedback effects turned on or off as they are using more precise visual cues and not steering wheel forces. If you are a sim racer, this is a great test to check whether you are driving more reactively or more predictively. If changing or turning off the FFB significantly affects your ability to drive, it's not the lack of a cue that is causing the problem. It's that you have a preprogrammed amount of steering force or rotation that you are used to applying. When the needed amount suddenly changes, how well can you adapt? The top drivers show very little difference and adjust quickly as they drive reacting to the correct cues, not using preprogrammed motions.

Not all hope for the steering wheel is lost though. There is some useful information to be had which we'll cover in a bit, but first let's look through all these forces we've talked about so far and see exactly what they are (and aren't) telling us.

Gaming cockpits such as the Obutto offer sim racers a stable platform to mount steering wheels, shifters, and pedals.

STEERING – TRAIL FORCES

The forces you feel through the steering wheel are directly related to the center of force at the contact patch and how far this is from the steering axis. The steering axis is an imaginary point on the ground that the tire rotates about. This point is almost always located in front of the contact patch for most vehicles. The distance between the two is called trail. The longer this trail distance, the more force you will feel on the steering wheel because it acts as a longer lever. This is why increasing caster makes steering heavier, as more positive caster increases trail.

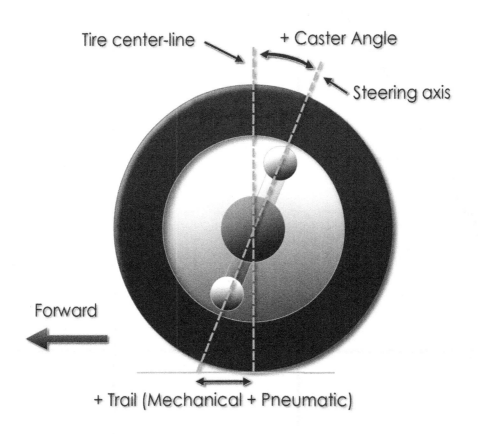

Tire center-line + Caster Angle

Steering axis

Forward

+ Trail (Mechanical + Pneumatic)

There is another part to this though, because you can actually separate trail into mechanical trail and pneumatic trail. Mechanical trail is the distance between these two points when the car is at rest, but the pneumatic trail changes as the tire twists and slides during cornering. This will either add or subtract from the total trail. As a tire approaches and goes past the limit, the center of force moves toward the front of the tire and so the lever arm acting on the steering wheel decreases. This will depend on the tire and the amount of mechanical trail, but you will sometimes feel some drop in steering force before you've reached the lateral grip limit of a tire. We say sometimes because it's often hard to feel this drop, as it's generally a pretty small effect compared to overall steering forces. There is also no way to know where in this lower steering force region the exact peak of grip actually is.

The most significant problem however, is that it's impossible to separate this drop off effect from the much greater effect on steering forces that load transfer and track features will have on the contact patch force. While you might be able to use the drop off effect to some degree on a smooth skidpad with pure lateral cornering, a racetrack corner will make it highly ineffective. During corner entry for example, as load is progressively transferring to the outside tire, you will have changes in tire loads that will have a direct effect on steering forces and there is no way for a driver to know if this is from a change in pneumatic trail or from a change in load. You will also have variations in load as you hit bumps and with changes in track elevation and banking. The center of force at the contact patch will also move around with different combinations of braking, throttle and steering, which will directly affect the trail length. An extreme example of this would be if you lock up the tires while trail braking. The direction of tire force will just move directly behind the steering axis and you will have a large drop off in steering forces as the self-centering effect of trail disappears. So in the end, although it offers some information in certain circumstances, this drop off effect from pneumatic trail is not a good way to determine grip limits even as a secondary cue and should most likely be ignored altogether.

STEERING – SCRUB RADIUS FORCES

Similar to the trail effect, but working in a sideways direction to the tire instead of front/back, we have steering forces caused by scrub radius. The scrub radius is the distance from the steering axis to the contact patch if you are looking at the tire from the front whereas trail is when you are looking at it from the side. It's important to understand however, that there is really only one steering axis and one contact patch, but splitting them laterally and longitudinally can help show you how tire forces from the two separate directions will affect your steering forces differently. While the trail will tell you about lateral forces, the scrub radius will tell you about longitudinal forces.

So what can these longitudinal forces tell us? Most significantly, they are going to tell us about single wheel bumps. If both front tires receive the same force, then they cancel each other out. If only one of your front tires hits a bump however, you **might** get a force at the steering wheel. We emphasize might because not all cars have a significant

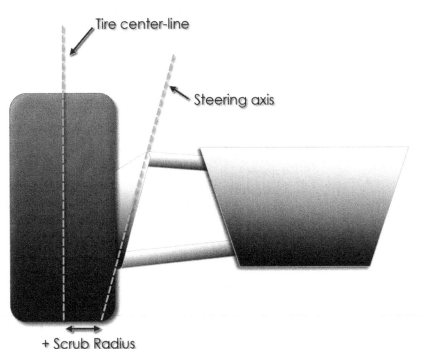

Tire center-line

Steering axis

+ Scrub Radius

scrub radius. If the suspension geometry has close to a zero scrub radius, the bump will have virtually no effect on steering. Usually a car has some amount of positive scrub radius however and you will get a force pulling the wheel in the direction of the bump. How much force you get depends on the length of the scrub radius and force from the bump. If you have a negative scrub radius, the force will actually push the steering wheel away from the bump. So are these steering forces from bumps a good thing? While each driver will have to decide for themselves, we would say no. If you hit a bump or curb, we think it is generally best if this doesn't have an effect on steering. Knowing where bumps and curbs are is good information, but you will still feel the bump through the chassis and even in sim racing you will see the bump affect the car. We feel however, that hitting a bump shouldn't cause an unwanted change in steering.

Another similar effect you will feel from scrub radius is with uneven braking force at the front wheels. This could be when you have one tire locking up under braking. You will feel the steering wheel pull to the side. The amount of force will be effected by the length of the scrub radius just as with the single wheel bumps. Knowing if you have tire lockup is very important information, but you will generally already be able to hear, and sometimes see the tire locking up, and more importantly, you should notice the effect this has on the car's movement. Just as with bumps, we don't want the steering affected. As an example why, if you are right by the edge of the track in the braking zone (as you generally should be) you don't want a sudden steering force to possibly make you drive off track.

Really all of this discussion of scrub radius is for information purposes only however. The amount and direction of these forces caused by scrub radius is set by the suspension geometry during the car design stage and can't usually be altered later by any significant amount. We primarily wanted to point out that this is another steering force that is not only imprecise, but possibly undesirable. This was also just a brief overview. There is a lot of info out there about trail, scrub radius, and steering forces if you wish to learn more.

STEERING FORCES – FINDING CENTER

Wow, steering forces are not looking so good are they? Is there any useful information we can gather from the steering wheel at all? Thankfully yes, while the steering forces won't tell us much about finding the maximum limits of grip, we can use them to find the minimum and that is more useful than it may seem at first.

A tire will always want to travel on the path of least resistance so it will create a force that wants to straighten the steering wheel to follow the direction the car is traveling. When you are driving in normal conditions or understeering at the limit, this will cause the steering to want to straighten out toward the center of the car. This is somewhat useful to keep the car from wandering on straights, but the real use of this centering force is when the car begins to oversteer excessively.

When a car is oversteering and a driver wants to correct, they need to either give the rear tires extra grip, take away grip from the front, or both. The common way to take away grip (reduce force) from the front is to countersteer far enough that car is traveling somewhat sideways though, the steering wheel would have a different "center" point. One of the easiest ways to find this new center is let the steering wheel tell you, as it will attempt to straighten itself in the direction the car is currently traveling.

You can use this cue to help control oversteer, but it usually is not without some driver intervention as well. In some cars, you can actually just let go of the steering wheel to correct oversteer, but sometimes, with severe oversteer you'll need to go past this new center point to not just remove any front force, but actually create force in the opposite direction and stop the excessive rotation speed. So while the steering wheel won't actually tell you the car is oversteering, it can be a help once you understand its use in controlling that oversteer.

STEERING POSITION

The final cue that you get from steering that we find quite useful actually has nothing to do with the forces at all. You can actually use the position and movement of the steering wheel to tell you a lot about how well you are doing in a corner. This cue is not really car control related though. It is more related to Line Theory.

You'll remember that during corner entry you are trying to get the car to turn as quickly as possible down to the apex. Done successfully, this creates a progressive turning of the wheel as you go through the spiral. The cue this gives us is that if you ever find yourself holding a steady steering position at corner entry then you are doing a slower, more circular entry. You should always see at least some progressive increase in steering during corner entry. This doesn't necessarily mean a constant smooth progression though. There might be some back and forth movement from testing and sometimes a quick oversteer correction will be needed, but as long as the average steering wheel trace shows a constant average increase in steering then you have a pretty good clue you are on the right track. We'll go into this in more detail during the driver input section, but wanted to introduce it here.

> You should always see at least some progressive increase in steering during corner entry.

TACTILE CUES – G FORCES

The final tactile cue and what many drivers consider the most important is g-forces, or more colloquially, the "seat of the pants" feeling. This is certainly a very useful cue and it can be an integral part of the Universal Cue if you know what to pay attention to. G-forces are not however, a necessary cue to achieve world-class performance. There are many very successful sim racing drivers who are able to turn near perfect laps on visual cues alone. There are also many real world drivers who take advantage of training on simulators lacking g-forces to improve their car control abilities out in the real world.

> G-force and visual cues are providing the exact same information.
>
> The information of movement.

The reason g-forces are useful, but not essential, is because they are only in support of visual cues. While the visual cues can be used in isolation, g-forces alone do not supply enough information.

But really, when we are talking about g-force cues, we are actually talking about a combination of g-force and visual cues as they are actually providing the exact same information. The information of movement.

G-forces are how we feel changes in movement. This can be movement in a certain direction or rotational movement. It's important to understand and be able to sense the distinction between these. Being able to sense the overall movement is what we call Universal Cue. The ability to sense rotation is what we call yaw sensitivity. We'll cover both of these more in depth shortly.

The way you experience this movement can be described through velocity, acceleration, and jerk. Velocity is simply the speed you are traveling. You can't actually feel velocity directly, although you can see it. Acceleration is a change in velocity. This is what you typically think of as g-forces and describes the constant force you feel during a turn. Unlike velocity, you can actually feel acceleration, but in itself, acceleration is not actually very useful. The most important of these movement terms is what is called jerk. Jerk is a change in acceleration and this is actually what you will be paying attention to as you drive.

If you remember from earlier in the book, car control is all about making a driver input change as a test to see if you get a change in car response. This change is a jerk. If you turn the steering wheel more and get an increase in lateral acceleration, you are sensing the jerk, the **change** in lateral acceleration. It is being able to sense the change that is important.

Again though, these movements are a visual as well as a tactile cue. If the car's movement changes, you can see it as well as feel it because they are both telling you the exact same thing. These also work together in that the more information your brain can take in, the easier it is to react to it. Stand on one foot with your eyes open and then closed. Most find this easier with their eyes open because of the additional information the brain receives.

There is no way to determine the exact relative importance of vision vs g-forces in this equation, but one area where vision is the clear winner is with sensing the **direction** of movement. You may be able to feel a change in movement, but only with your eyes can you see where that movement is taking you. As we've learned, the direction of force, and thus movement, is ultimately what is most important. So now that we understand how important visual cues are in the overall picture, let's take a look at those.

VISUAL CUES - BEYOND LOOKING AHEAD

One of the first pieces of advice many new drivers hear is to "look ahead." It's interesting that you should have to remind someone to look where they are going as it seems pretty obvious, but just like in our crazy parking lot car from the beginning of the book, if you are focusing all of your attention on controlling your car, you don't have much left over to focus on where you are going.

On the flipside though, if you are focusing on finding the perfect apex on track, you don't have much attention left to focus on your car control. So really, where you place your focus needs to be an intelligent decision based on what your current goals are. During training, while your primary goal is on improving your car control, having more focus on the car will be necessary. Your focus would be on improving your car control abilities, not using a track to its absolute limits where looking ahead into a corner is paramount. This is easier if you can do it in an environment that supports safe experimentation like autocross or sim racing, but even on a normal track, you can accomplish the same thing by giving yourself a good margin of error by staying away from the edges of the track.

While looking ahead certainly has its place in racing situations when you are trying to minimize lap times, there are no absolutes, and it's more important to understand when and why you should focus on looking ahead so you can make that decision intelligently. Also we aren't saying focusing on car control means looking at the hood of the car or steering wheel or something like that. You should still be looking out at the track, the primary difference is on where your attention and focus primarily lies.

One issue many drivers have however, is that as their car control skills improve, they are so accustomed to focusing on the car to keep it under control at the limit that it's hard for them to transition back to looking ahead. Because of this tendency, you might have to actually start thinking about your eyes as a driver input. As you approach a braking point, your eyes should move to start searching for the apex. As you approach the apex, your eyes should be searching for the limits of the track where you predict your corner exit will take you. This might have to be an actual conscious movement that will need to be trained. If you ever find yourself missing an apex or trackout point by a good bit, the culprit is almost always going to be that you weren't looking for it in time. Not a lack of car control.

Eventually, as your car control skills improve and become more automatic, almost all your focus will not simply be on just looking ahead, but actually visualizing everything about where you are in relation to the entire corner. Having great spatial awareness and sensitivity to movement is the hallmark of a great driver and if you wish to develop this sensitivity in yourself, you will need to learn the two visual (and g-force) based cues that offer ultimate precision. The precision that can only come from directly following the physics of racing, the science of movement. These two cues are yaw sensitivity and The Universal Cue. These are the primary cues to pay attention to as you drive.

First up, yaw sensitivity will be the primary way that a driver controls car balance and is the very essence of car control. So what exactly is yaw sensitivity? Yaw sensitivity is **the ability to detect changes in the rate of rotation**. If you sit in an office chair and someone spins you around, being able to see and feel the changes in rotation speed with each push is yaw sensitivity. Its primary use is to detect understeer and oversteer. A car that is tightening its turning radius will have an increase in rotation speed and if the radius is widening it will be decreasing its rotation speed.

> Yaw sensitivity is the ability to detect changes in the rate of rotation.

YAW SENSITIVITY – DETECTING **UNDERSTEER** & **OVERSTEER**

We define understeer as when a car reaches the limit of grip of the front tires before the rear. Some people think understeer only means that a car has started to plow off the track, but while a car is most certainly understeering in a situation like that, you might also be understeering the entire way through a perfectly executed corner. This is because, as we mentioned earlier, for ultimate speed you need to be at the very limit of the tires and either understeering and/or oversteering the entire way through a corner.

The key is that if you are understeering in a corner, you should be at the limit, but just barely. The way you keep the car at this bare minimum understeer is through yaw sensitivity. Imagine you are driving through a corner at what you think might be the limit. How can you know for sure? How do you find out if there is any more grip left to use or if you've already gone past the limit and are sliding? Do you listen to the tires? Do you feel it through the steering wheel?

No. You must test. You must turn the steering wheel more and see if the car increases its rate of rotation. **If this increases your rotation rate, you were not at the limit, and if it doesn't, you are at or over the limit**. Simple as that. A driver can see as well as feel this change in rotation speed. This is a precise cue because we are directly determining if we can generate any more force. We are not using any imprecise secondary cues such as tire noises or steering wheel forces. We are going straight to the actual physics.

> Turn the steering wheel more and see if the car increases its rate of rotation. If this increases your rotation rate, you were not at the limit, and if it doesn't, you are at or over the limit.

In practice, this will look like constant movements of the steering wheel as the driver aims to keep the tires right at the limit without going over. The better a driver's yaw sensitivity, the smaller these movements can be, but they must always be there if the driver wants to **know** if they are truly at the limit and not over or under it.

For a beginning driver these movements might need to be larger as you must actually detect a change in rotation or lack thereof in response to your steering. This may require a big movement if you are not very sensitive to yaw yet. Some novice drivers may try to mimic the smaller, precise movements of more advanced drivers, but unless the steering movements they are making are actually a response, then they are usually just making the car wiggle through the corner under the limit. The car should not be doing any wiggling if you are near the peak of grip. If the car has a big rotational response to your testing movement, it means you aren't near the limit.

While there will also be at least some effect on the car's overall movement from the steering change that you can detect with the Universal Cue, for car control purposes, it's usually easier to detect the change in yaw velocity (rotation). Yaw sensitivity gives you direct feedback of the car's current front vs rear grip levels. Sometimes the car will start rotating faster or slower without an initial noticeable change in overall movement. The driver will be able to detect the rotational change sooner with yaw sensitivity, and this becomes especially important for detecting oversteer.

Oversteer occurs when the rear tires reach the limit before the front tires do. Using yaw sensitivity to detect oversteer is then naturally the opposite of detecting understeer. A driver will detect oversteer because of an increase in rotation rate without an equivalent increase in steering. Another way to think of this is that a car is in oversteer if the driver is **unable** to reach understeer. For example, if an increase in steering never causes the car to **stop** rotating faster (understeer) and instead the rotation rate begins accelerating as the rear tires go past the limit, the car is oversteering. Although it is certainly more difficult, it is still possible to drive at the limit of the rear tires in constant oversteer. We're not talking about drifting though. Drifting is where you have significant oversteer with the rear tires way past the limit and the driver is using a lot of counter-steering to control it. We're talking about controlled driving at the limit of the rear tires. Someone watching this might not be able to tell the car is in oversteer because from the outside it would look basically the same as an understeering car. The driver would know however, because the small testing movements in steering or throttle would cause an accelerated rotation rate from oversteer instead of the lack of rotation that indicates understeer.

In practice, oversteer is usually caused by some sort of driver input, sometimes on purpose and sometimes not. Very few cars are setup to begin oversteering if the limit is approached smoothly. If a car does start to oversteer however, and the driver wishes to correct, they would typically reduce steering and may also alter brake or throttle to balance the car before they have excessive, possibly uncatchable oversteer.

If an increase in steering never causes your rotation rate to stop rising (understeer) and instead the rotation rate begins accelerating, the car is oversteering.

Controlling oversteer is about finding the balance point at the limit of the rear tires and to a certain extent this comes naturally. You can even sometimes see children for the first time in a kart naturally countersteer in response to the rear coming out. The steering wheel movements to test for and control oversteer will look very similar to the movements for understeer, but sometimes they can be a bit faster. If you have a sudden large oversteer from a bump or some other large disturbance you will need a large, fast steering wheel movement to catch the car. If however, you are getting only a little bit of oversteer from throttle application, you might have smaller steering wheel movements to keep the rear in check.

This testing/correction can also be done with the pedals as well though. For example, during corner exit with a car that will readily go into power oversteer, you must balance the steering and throttle together to keep the tires at the limit as best you can. If you zoomed in on a steering/throttle trace, this will many times look like a stair-step movement of steering and throttle. A move, pause, move, pause. A driver that tests more with the throttle might have a smoother steering movement and more of a variation in throttle movement. A driver that tests more with steering would have the opposite. There would also be a similar testing process balancing steering and brakes during corner entry.

Understand though, just as when testing for understeer, oversteer correction and yaw sensitivity is really just about balance. Controlling the front vs rear grip level by sensing how the car's rotation rate is affected by driver inputs. There is no precise procedure. This explanation of testing/correction should just be a general guide. It's probably not a good idea to over-intellectualize how exactly your hands and feet should move. Just like learning to walk a tightrope, the proper movements will come naturally if you understand the cues to pay attention to. After a spin, students will sometimes ask their instructor what they did wrong, but the real answer is that they simply lost their balance. If a tightrope walker falls off, they normally don't ask how they should have shifted their weight better. They get back up on the tightrope and keep working on improving their balance. It just takes a lot of practice to be able to balance the rear of the car at the limit, but it is worth the effort because using the maximum grip the rear tires can provide increases the total tire force you can generate.

So in the end, yaw sensitivity is simply about balance. Just like tight tope walking, it's a skill you will slowly build up over the years if you train properly and constantly push your limits. You will eventually be able to drive any car consistently to its limits. But will you be a champion? Will you be breaking track records? Not necessarily. Because although having great car control is essential for speed, it's not quite enough. To reach true world-class levels, you have to start looking elsewhere.

THE **UNIVERSAL CUE**

Introduced at the end of *The Perfect Corner* we are finally getting back to the Universal Cue we talk so much about. This is the big one that eventually will be the primary cue that a driver should follow. While having great yaw sensitivity can give you amazing control over the car, it doesn't tell you exactly what you should be doing with that control. To determine that, you need an understanding of Line Theory and then combine that knowledge with the Universal Cue to optimize your movement through a corner.

If yaw sensitivity is the ability to detect changes in rotation, the **Universal Cue is the ability to detect changes in overall movement**. For example, if you would use yaw sensitivity to detect someone spinning you in an office chair, the Universal Cue would allow you to detect your change in movement and acceleration as they pushed you around the room. You will need to be able to detect and differentiate both of these types of movement and then use this information to optimize the forces the tires are applying to the car.

Any force on a freely moving object will cause an acceleration and thus movement. If you throw a ball in the air, there is a constant downward force and acceleration from gravity. We can see how it affects the ball's path and predict it. How does a good ball player know where a ball is going to go almost as soon as it is kicked or thrown? If gravity randomly changed and the ball didn't have a constant downward acceleration, this would be impossible.

If there are even small changes in a ball's normal trajectory because of wind or other factors, it makes it harder to predict, but a good player can see these changes happen very quickly and react to them. They are very sensitive to changes in the path the ball takes. They are detecting the movement in the same way a driver detects movement with the Universal Cue. Are you starting to understand why we call it the **Universal** Cue?

40 | P a g e

Of course, a racecar driver must be able to detect these change while in the car, not from the outside, so while the principle is universal, developing this skill is not. Watching balls fly through the air won't help you drive a car any faster. To help you wrap your head around this concept we're going to tell another little story now. No cannibal marauders this time though. Just a driver and his grandmother.

Any performance driver has probably had the experience of driving a loved one somewhere only to be berated for driving too fast despite the fact we know we are very far from the limit. Our driver in this story has been tasked with taking his grandmother to her weekly bingo match. As they near a stop sign, the driver is faced with a similar problem to what a racecar driver faces as they approach a corner. He must predict when he needs to begin applying the brakes so that they arrive at the stop sign without exceeding the limit. As he learned on their last trip to bingo, the limit in this case is about .05 g before their grandmother starts to fuss about how her grandson is trying to kill her.

Our driver will begin applying brakes with the goal of staying right at the grandmother limit of .05 g so that they arrive at the stop sign just as they reach 0 mph. They don't want to exceed the limit, but they also don't want to start braking too early or they are wasting time, which no performance driver wants to do. They must predict the distance it will take for their car to stop. As they slow down, they must have constant awareness of their current speed, deceleration, and distance to the stop sign. They will be modulating brake pressure so as to minimize the time to the stop sign while ideally not going over the grandmother limit.

The driver probably doesn't realize it, but they are using the Universal Cue. If they were sensitive to the cue, they would be able to see and feel their deceleration rate accurately so as to remain below the limit while also minimizing the time to reach the stop sign. If they were insensitive to the Universal Cue, they wouldn't know how close to this limit they were until grandma started yelling. They would be using the grandma yelling cue and because this is not a very precise cue, they would need to play it safe and brake earlier to give themselves extra time and distance. This lack of sensitivity and earlier braking might even cause them to have to speed back up a little at some point during the process if they significantly over-slowed.

Of course, while if our driver exceeds the (grandmother) limit they have to deal with an irate relative, a racecar driver that exceeds the (grip) limit will miss their apex. But in both cases, the alternative of playing it safe leads to lost time. A racecar driver must therefore be able to predict the maximum force their car will be able to generate to push them in the ideal direction at each section of the upcoming corner and what path this maximized force will carry them on. This is a good bit harder than driving grandmother to bingo, but the principle is the same. Every driver already at least somewhat uses this ability to track their movement as they drive. We talk a lot about the Universal Cue and try to explain it in several different ways, because while intellectually it can be a very simple concept, it can sometimes be hard for drivers to put it into practice. A driver may be curious how sensitive they are to the cue or wonder how to know if they are improving at it.

We think the best way to check yourself is to essentially reverse engineer it. Remember, the goal of Line Theory is basically to get from point A to point B in the minimum time possible so you'll know you are improving your Universal Cue sensitivity when you become better at predicting your sector times. The more variables you can isolate the better, so setting your sector to just one corner is ideal. If you felt you were able to maximize the car's tire forces to push you in the ideal direction better than you had all session and then your time reflects that, you know it's because of your sensitivity to the cue.

If you can make this prediction regularly, you know you are getting sensitive to the Universal Cue because no other cue can so accurately give you this information. We're not going to lie and say this is easy, but if you understand why this is the only true answer, it makes it easier to take on this challenge because you'll also understand the rewards that await you.

SHORTCUT **CUES**

Although they aren't as accurate, sometimes there are other ways besides the Universal Cue to determine the fastest way through a corner. Essentially a shortcut to determine the optimal line. Whether or not there is a shortcut will depend primarily on which wheels are driven and the relative power compared to grip levels of a vehicle. We'll cover all the shortcuts in their respective sections later on, but a quick example would be a rear-wheel drive car that naturally understeers during corner exit. This is actually a fairly common situation and it has a great, easy to use shortcut where you can quickly determine an optimal corner exit before you've developed your sensitivity to the Universal Cue.

The shortcut in this case is to use maximum throttle from the apex while using yaw sensitivity to keep the car as close to the limit of understeer as possible. This is actually a very precise way to do corner exit properly in a car like this and done well you don't actually need the Universal Cue at all until you are trying to find that last little bit of speed. Shortcuts are important because increasing sensitivity to overall car movement can be hard in the beginning when you have to focus so much on just keeping the car under control. Using a shortcut where all you have to do is focus on one aspect of car control while simply making sure you use the whole track can take you far.

Some racing situations provide no real shortcuts though. This is very prevalent in cars that are either front-wheel drive or 4-wheel drive with enough power or low enough traction to spin the tires at will. We'll explain why later in the book, but in these situations, the Universal Cue is the **only** thing you have to go by to determine your optimum corner. This might be a big reason rally drivers are so successful in competitions like the Race of Champions where quickly adapting to a wide variety of cars is important. Off-road drivers must be very sensitive to overall car movement to drive effectively.

SELF-EVALUATING WITH THE UNIVERSAL CUE

While the Universal Cue is used actively while in a corner to control a car, as we mentioned it's also the best way for a driver to self-evaluate their performance and determine how well they've optimized a corner. If they were able to maximize the car's movement in the ideal direction throughout the entire corner, they know that it's optimized. We've seen drivers who are very good at this and can accurately predict their sector times to within a 20th of a second. They almost always know when they've just done their best lap without looking at their times. This is because there is no other cue you can use to track your performance as well. As we learned in *The Perfect Corner,* you can't look at corner exit speed or apex speed to do anything beyond find out if you are in the ballpark. Even following just yaw sensitivity, which is a precise cue, won't give you the information you need to determine performance. You can keep the car right at the limit and get on the throttle right at the apex, but if the tire forces aren't pushing you in the ideal direction, your times could still vary by a few 10ths in the corner. If you've ever felt like you did really great in a corner, but your times didn't reflect it, this is the reason. You were paying attention to the wrong cues.

IDEAL DIRECTION

The ideal direction follows the angle of the track during corner entry and exit. Therefore, in a 180-degree corner such as the Suzuka Hairpin, the ideal direction remains the same after the apex

SIM RACING CUE CONSIDERATIONS

So how does the Universal Cue translate to sim racing where all g-forces are missing? Well, this does make it harder to sense, but vision alone does provide all the movement information you need. Plus, the handicap of having no supporting g-forces can be a fantastic training opportunity. Some sim drivers, in an attempt to compensate for what they feel they are losing without the "seat of the pants" feeling focus on other less precise cues such as tire noises or steering forces. They might use view modifications that try to show yaw and g-forces through other means in an attempt to help with driving a car in the simulated environment.

None of this is necessary however, as yaw sensitivity and the Universal Cue should ideally still be your main cues even when sim racing. While adding real life g-forces certainly helps, it's absolutely not required and top sim racers can drive near perfect laps on visual cues alone.

> Sim drivers are not at any disadvantage and can follow along with these cues with confidence that they will transfer to sim racing as well as real racing.

While you do feel changes in movement through g-force cues, you also must use your vision and spatial awareness to know exactly where in the corner you are and which direction the tire forces are pushing you. Without that additional visual information, the tactile cues alone are meaningless. Losing the additional depth perception by going to a monitor or TV is probably more of a hindrance to your spatial awareness than losing your g-force cues. Newer virtual reality 3D options for simulators can somewhat rectify this depth perception problem though.

PART 2 - DRIVER INPUTS

So far, we've learned a lot about what the car can tell us, but how do we put all this to use? To drive reactively, we must react. We must do something in response to these cues we've learned. We've touched on some of these briefly, but the remainder of this book will focus on how the cues work together with the driver inputs and how to optimize this relationship. While for the vast majority of vehicles, the primary driver inputs are the throttle, brakes, and steering wheel, the way we use these will change depending on where we are in the corner, the car's capabilities, and whether the car is under or oversteering.

First, we are going to divide a corner into the deceleration and acceleration phases as well as cover the very important transition phase as you go between the two. We will also look at a simple way to understand the tire forces that are created by our driver inputs and how to use them optimally. Finally, we will further break each phase down into understeer and oversteer control. We'll see how a car's basic capabilities will determine whether we will ideally be understeering or oversteering during the different corner phases. Before we get to all that though, let's look at a few more common misconceptions dealing with car control.

STEERING

BRAKES   THROTTLE

BEYOND SMOOTH

One of the most common pieces of advice that drivers often hear is to be smooth. Smooth is fast. While this advice is not wrong, it's often misunderstood. Some drivers hear this advice and they will focus on just making their inputs as smooth as possible. We've learned however, that ideally we want our inputs to be a reaction to the proper car control cues. A driver focusing on their inputs alone may look smooth, but it is only because they are not pushing the car's limits, and therefore their lap times will suffer. Most importantly however, they aren't improving their car control skills, their **reactive** driving ability. If you want to achieve your best performance, you have to start looking beyond simply trying to be smooth.

In order to improve core car control abilities, a driver must learn to drive based on cues (reactively). This may cause them to at first be slower and look sloppier than a driver just focusing on smooth inputs, but because they are constantly pushing their ability to drive at the limits, they will eventually get faster **and** smoother.

Or rather, they will be able to make the car look incredibly smooth, as it will have no sudden changes in rotation speed or acceleration. If you looked at their driver inputs however, there is usually always small quick corrections as they are constantly reacting to cues and testing the limits of grip. They are not just trying to be smooth, they are trying to be as fast as possible and a smooth looking car and minimal driver inputs are the result. Sometimes the inputs are smooth, and sometimes they aren't. The driver inputs simply need to be whatever keeps the car right at the limit going in the ideal direction.

> Every single input a driver makes should be on purpose, a reaction.

While top drivers do look very smooth, this is only because of excellent, hard-earned car control skills. If you wish to improve long-term, you will need to push your reactive driving abilities to the limits. Don't try to fake the smoothness you see from advanced drivers or you will just hamper your progress.

Rather than just trying to be smooth, every single input a driver makes should be on purpose, a reaction. While you will certainly improve your predictive driving with a car/track combo and be able to use your predictions to get close, there is no way to ever know and preplan exactly what inputs will be needed at any instant. Reactive driving will always need to be there as a final layer for ultimate performance.

Let's look at a quick example of why you ideally want to drive based on cues and not just using preplanned motions. You often hear that you should roll on the throttle smoothly. If there is novice driver that is thoughtlessly slamming on the throttle, someone might recommend they try to focus on making their pedal application smoother. This sounds like good advice because if a driver isn't paying attention to what they are doing, they are better off just doing it smoothly by focusing on the driver input. But ideally, the novice driver should learn to focus not on their input, but on the proper cues and then reactively apply the throttle as quickly as possible.

The speed with which they should apply throttle will be determined by many factors, but the result of going too far will always be either excessive understeer or oversteer which will be detected through a cue. In this case, yaw sensitivity. The result of doing it too slowly by arbitrarily rolling on the throttle however, will be lost time. If a driver only focuses on the input without paying attention to cues, they are giving up potential time that a more sensitive driver could find. It may initially be harder to drive reactively, but if you find yourself just focusing on making a driver input smoothly without reacting to a cue, you are probably not only losing time, but also not improving.

Furthering this point, it's rarely the speed with which a driver makes an input that causes a problem, but rather that they are making an excessive input in the first place. The speed with which a car can accept a driver input is only going to be limited by how quickly the load transfers. The greater the load on a tire, the more grip it has, so if a driver tries to use the maximum grip a tire would generate at full load before the load has gotten there, the tire will go past the limit. While this is a very real effect, in almost any type of competitively prepared car, you are rarely going to be making an input too fast for the load transfer unless that input was simply too much in the first place. In short, the problem is usually not that a driver did something too fast, they most likely just did the wrong thing.

A great example of this is with brake release. You often hear that you must be smooth with your brake release. That you must "time" your release to allow the suspension to respond and if you pop off the brakes quickly, you will create oversteer. This is a very real effect, but is usually relatively small as the load transfers fast enough in most performance oriented cars that, by itself, the brake release won't cause oversteer unless the car was already going to oversteer anyway. For example, if you have a very stable car that always understeers during trail braking because of its setup, a driver most likely won't be able to cause oversteer even if they let off the brakes as fast as they can. The effect of load transfer speed on balance is just too small. For a driver to get oversteer in this situation, the cause is usually the much more powerful effect of yaw inertia, which we'll cover shortly.

The primary way that brake release will cause oversteer comes from when a car has a more performance oriented neutral setup. For this type of setup, there is generally going to be some combination of tire forces caused by trail braking that will initiate oversteer if the car is driven at the limit during corner entry. So if a driver in a neutrally balanced car goes into a corner too fast for their abilities, there is a high probability they might spin if they are at the limit and let off the brakes to that oversteering tire force combination.

The problem was not that they let off the brakes too quickly however. They would have spun regardless unless they had the skill to control the oversteer caused by the input combination. This driver might then be taught that they should smoothly release the brakes, because to combat this corner entry oversteer, many drivers will learn the tendencies of their car and if there is always an input combination that induces oversteer, they will often essentially skip it by dropping below the limit as they go through it. This is commonly done by smoothly releasing the brakes and over-slowing a bit to go past this point slightly under the limit. This does work to prevent corner entry oversteer, but only because the driver is not at the limit. It focuses on timing the driver input, not on reacting to a cue and the driver is losing potential time.

There is nothing wrong with this solution for a more novice driver in a race situation however, as the ideal solution can be significantly harder. We'll cover the ideal solution shortly, but right now primarily just wanted to point out that corner entry oversteer issues, and most other handling issues are rarely cause by the speed of a driver input. They are generally caused by the wrong input. Later in the book, we'll look at an easy way to visualize how the tire force amounts and directions affect balance and you'll see why corner entry oversteer can be such a problem.

The takeaway point from all this is that you shouldn't ever feel like you should simply release the brakes slowly or just smoothly make any driver input. Sometimes you will want to do things slowly and sometimes very quickly. It's more important to react to the proper car control cues. If your car actually is oversteering because of brake release speed and not because of the input combination or yaw inertia, then only paying attention to your cues will tell you this.

YAW INERTIA

Yaw inertia is the tendency for a car to continue rotating at the same speed. It doesn't want to increase or decrease its rotation rate (yaw velocity.) This can cause a big, heavy car to be unresponsive during turn-in, but more of a problem is that it can also cause a car to want to continue rotating at the apex when you ideally want to start reversing that rotation rate. This is the basis behind the Scandinavian Flick in rally driving where it is used on purpose to initiate oversteer. This can still happen in normal race driving as well however, but is usually almost never desired.

A typical situation where yaw inertia can be a problem is when a novice driver first starts reaching the limit. Unlike an advanced driver that drives the entire corner at the limit and has a steady increase/decrease in rotation rate, the novice driver will often begin the corner under the limit and then turn in more and more until they reach the limit somewhere in the middle of the turn. This results in a faster than ideal rotation rate right as they reach the apex where they need to start reversing that rotation. Combine this with the imprecise driver inputs of a novice and even a very understeering car might spin. Just as we mentioned before, it wasn't that the speed of the steering input was too fast for the load transfer. The driver simply created more yaw velocity than they were able to control. This can happen in softly sprung or very stiff cars regardless of how quickly the load transfers. The relatively small balance effect added in if this driver popped off the brakes would simply be the nail in the coffin.

Even if a car is driven perfectly however, yaw inertia can be an issue in certain corner combinations. The transition in the middle of a chicane can create yaw accelerations that almost exactly mimic the Scandinavian Flick. A driver will need to determine if their car can handle the ideal transition speed or if they might need to compromise the speed of transition somewhat so that they don't create uncontrollable yaw velocity that could lead to a spin.

YAW SENSITIVITY- A DRIVER'S EYE VIEW

We've talked a lot about yaw and being able to sense changes in rotation, but let's look a little more at how this works from the driver's point of view. How a skilled driver can jump into virtually any vehicle and determine how to get the maximum performance out of it simply by driving reactively based on its understeer and oversteer limits. We've mentioned multiple times the concept that every driver input should be a reaction to a cue. You don't need different techniques that you must preprogram and memorize for every different car and corner. This principle of reacting to oversteer and understeer cues allows you to dispense with a whole plethora of specific circumstance-based driving techniques. Again, you never want to **time** a steering input, brake release, or throttle application. The concept of timing something is not based on a car control cue because **time** is not a cue. Memorizing a way to do something based on timing is just one solution for one specific circumstance.

Let's look again at throttle application as an example of how using yaw sensitivity alone provides the proper technique. Imagine we have a very low-powered car and an understeering setup that allows us to apply throttle very quickly as we pass the apex. The driver would use their yaw sensitivity testing to know they were understeering at that point and feel that the understeer continued as the throttle was applied at the apex. They would then try to keep it right at the understeer limit through the rest of the corner.

What if however, that same car had a more neutral setup? It could be right at the limit of oversteer at throttle application and as the driver applied throttle, the car would start to oversteer a little. To avoid excessive oversteer, the driver would have to slow their throttle input as they removed a little bit of steering before going to full throttle. They would then keep the car as close to the oversteer (or understeer) limit as possible through the rest of the corner. In both situations, the driver used their yaw sensitivity to drive reactively and keep the car as close to the limit as possible, but due to the different car setups, the driver inputs needed and end result turned out differently. We can apply this same principle to all throttle application situations. What if you had a powerful car that could spin the rear tires and oversteer easily? Or there was a big bump in the track at the apex? Both of these things would affect the car's balance, but the driver's reaction would always be the same. They would attempt to maximize acceleration while using yaw sensitivity to stay as close as possible to the oversteer and/or understeer limit. If in any of these situations, the driver had simply applied the throttle smoothly or done any other number of preprogrammed timed actions they would probably be losing time. Again though, they would have no way of knowing because they weren't driving based on cues.

All other handling situations follow this exact same principle as well. If a driver has developed their yaw sensitivity to very high levels, they can jump into any car, on any track and very quickly know how to drive it to its maximum limits only by being able to detect when it reaches understeer and oversteer. We'll be delving into the driver inputs needed to do this shortly.

The Race of Champions is a head-to-head competition of the best drivers in the world where quickly adapting to a wide variety of cars is the key to victory.

THE (UN)IMPORTANCE OF **LOAD TRANSFER**

Before we move on to these driver inputs though, we wanted to look at one final popular driving misconception. That is the importance to the driver, or rather lack thereof, of load transfer. We are not saying that load transfer is not a very real and important effect. Understanding load transfer is essential for car setup as it explains a good many things about why a car behaves in a certain manner. But from the driver's perspective, it's actually of very little importance despite what you may often hear. It's actually not the load transfer that is important to the driver, it's the direction of force generated by the tires that is. The load transfer is simply a side effect of that.

Let's go through an example with another common piece of advice so we can look at this more in depth. You often hear that during corner entry, you should apply the brakes to transfer load to the front so the tires have more grip and will turn better. This is a somewhat correct conclusion, but the reasoning is flawed. It's not actually the load transfer to the front that makes a car turn faster. As we learned in *The Perfect Corner,* applying the brakes changes the direction of force the tires are generating to a more optimized direction for turning. It's actually this change in direction of force that causes the car to tighten its entry spiral. The load transfer is simply a reaction to this change in force. The more force the driver can generate, the greater the load transfer will be.

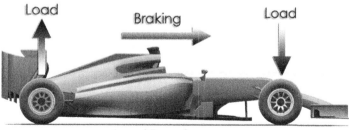

Load   Braking   Load

Load Transfer

Ironically, an increase in load transfer to the front tires will actually reduce our ability to turn. If you raise the center of gravity of a car, you will create more load transfer for the same amount of braking force. Because of tire load sensitivity, this will reduce the overall grip and thus force the car can produce and will cause you to reduce your radius slower than before. All four tires generate braking and turning forces, so due to this tire load sensitivity, the more evenly spread the load is, the greater overall force you can produce. If only the front wheels had brakes, you would actually get an increase in turning with more load transfer, but we've never heard of a car that only had brakes on the front. We're not going to get into the science of load sensitivity in this book, but there is a lot of publicly available information out there for those curious.

So although load transfer does change the grip levels and balance of a car, it is not something that a driver should try and directly manipulate. In other words, you shouldn't make a driver input with the goal of trying to add or remove load from a tire. A driver should instead focus on generating the maximum force the car can provide to push them in the ideal direction. The load transfer is simply a side effect of this force. There isn't really anything outside of a setup change that a driver can do to modify load transfer to improve their performance.

> Although load transfer changes the grip levels and balance of a car, it is not something that a driver should try and directly manipulate.

Now that we've looked at a few misconceptions, let's start looking at some real answers. We talk a lot about force direction because that is the only thing that truly determines your final lap time. As we learned earlier, these forces are generated at the tire/track interaction so let's take a closer look at a tire now to see how these forces originate and how a driver can learn to manipulate them.

TIRE FORCES SIMPLIFIED

Many drivers are aware of the concept of a traction circle. It represents the fact that a tire can only generate a certain amount of force in any one direction at a time. A good way to visualize this as seen on the opposite page is a circle drawn on the track going around the tire. This circle would grow or shrink based on the changing grip from the amount of load currently on the tire. The outside of the circle represents the maximum possible grip the tire can generate at that instant.

We can then draw a line from the center of the tire outward. This represents the current amount and direction of force that the tire is trying to push the car in. Note that this is the actual direction the tire is currently trying to move and take the car with it. The further out the arrow goes toward the edge, the more force it is generating. If the line reaches the edge of the circle, the tire is at the limit of traction. The line cannot go outside the circle. We'll explain shortly what happens if a driver attempts to make it do so.

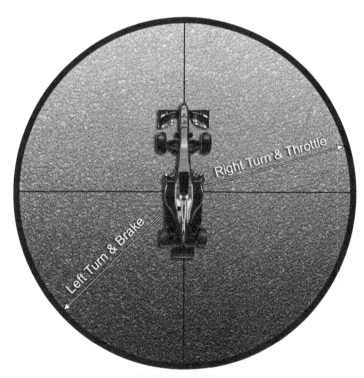

All four tires' individual traction circles combine to create one traction circle originating from the car's center of gravity.

STEERING **FORCES**

Let's first consider how this looks in a pure steering situation. If you have a car going at a constant speed and the driver then steadily increased the steering, the force line would start at the center of the tire and move quickly outward, but angled slightly toward the rear of the car until it reached the outside of the circle at the limit of traction. We've shown three arrows representing tire forces at the peak grip and then while sliding, but at any instant, the arrow would simply follow the curved line as the tire turned more in relation to the track.

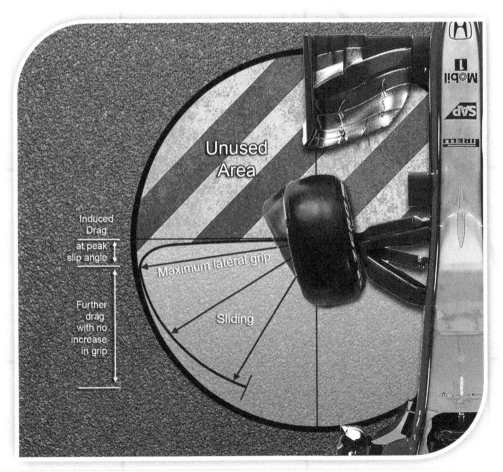

The exact shape of the curve would depend on the tire construction, but the illustration shows what a typical tire would do. Ideally, we would want the arrow to go straight out to the side, just giving us pure lateral force as we turned the steering wheel, but even with no brakes applied, our tire force line will always have some deceleration force as well. This rearward movement of the force line is called induced drag and is very important to take into account. At the point of peak lateral grip where the arrow is as far laterally as it's going to get, there is already a fair amount of drag. This is caused by partial sliding of the contact patch and the twisting of the tire carcass under load. In general, the stiffer the tire is, the less induced drag there will be. The part labeled unused area shows how the tire will never generate force in that area. It will never be completely sideways because of induced drag or forward because this is not a 4-wheel drive car.

As you can see, if the driver continued to turn the wheel past the peak of grip, the force line would pull in from the edge of the circle and follow it around toward the rear of the car until you hit the maximum steering lock. It doesn't stay on the outside of the circle because you are past the grip peak at this point and the tire is completely sliding. This generates extra heat in the tire as well as diminished force.

More importantly though, we can tell from the circle that it reduces the lateral force and starts to act more and more like applying the brakes as it is trying to push the tire and car backwards from its current direction of travel. An important takeaway here is that anytime a tire generates lateral grip, even a tiny amount, there will always be at least some rearward drag force that acts just like using brakes. The amount of this will vary based on the tire, but the drag forces a tire generates at its peak of grip are not insignificant and adding to this induced drag by steering more than necessary can be very harmful to lap times.

So how would all this look from the viewpoint of the driver? While driving at a constant speed, as they turn the steering wheel more and more, the driver will experience all this as a steady increase in turning rate until the rate tapers off as they

Power Oversteer

Understeer

reach the peak. This is the maximum grip the tire can provide and the car will not be able to corner any faster. If the driver continues to turn the wheel however, the lateral force will diminish and rearward force will increase. To the driver they will see this as the car initially widening its arc from the loss in lateral force and then beginning to slow down as the line heads more and more rearward and acts like brakes. Even if the actual maximum tire grip doesn't diminish much after the peak (it's still fairly close to the edge of the circle), the lateral turning force will still continue to decrease as the steering is turned because the line is heading toward the rear of the car and away from the side where it was generating lateral force.

It's also important to understand that any lateral force generated by the front tire is transmitted to the rear tire as well. It is not only the front tires that provide turning forces. We can visualize this by simply copying the current lateral force from the front to the rear tire. This illustration shows that the rear circle is larger than the front. This does not necessarily mean that it has more load on it however.

The larger rear circle is depicting a car that would understeer at the limit in pure cornering when no braking or throttle is being applied. Most cars are set up this way. As load is transferred forward and backward from deceleration and acceleration forces, the circles will grow and shrink respectively, potentially altering balance. But right now, in pure cornering mode, we can see the front tire is just right at the limit of traction pushing the car sideways. We then create a line going directly backwards from this point where it passes through the rear circle.

Since the rear tires aren't doing anything else right now, they will respond to the tire force sent back and provide their own force line going out to meet the one from the front. The circle is larger at the rear, which means it has more capacity than the front to generate grip, and so the car will understeer at the limit. Remember, the front tire is already at the limit so it can't generate any more force to push the line further out that is sent back to the rear circle. Also note that the rear tire will have induced drag just like the front.

It's not really the circles that matter for balance though, it's the lines. If the line at the front ever goes further out from the car than the line at the rear, the car will start to oversteer. This can happen because of load transfer, which changes the relative circle sizes, as well as by throttle and brake forces which will take up some of the circle and limit the lateral force capacity. An example of this is shown by the line labeled power oversteer. We'll look at these throttle and brake forces shortly.

We want to note that this is not technically how car balance works, as we are combining the front and rear tire pair for simplicity. You actually have to look at all four tires as a torque about the center of gravity of the car. This method is a very close approximation however, and it works well for explanation purposes in this book.

BRAKING **FORCES**

Now let's add in some braking forces. A good way to think of braking forces is that they can override the steering forces. A tire creates a steering force because of its ability to roll freely, but as you remove that ability with brakes, the tire has less lateral force capability.

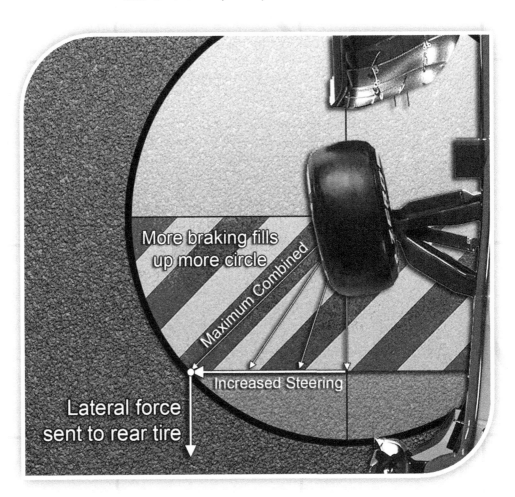

For example, if you were at the limit in pure cornering and go to maximum brakes, the line on the traction circle would immediately go inwards and back. The tire will lose all lateral capacity and the tire force will simply point in the opposite direction from where the car is traveling to make it slow down.

Conversely, if you are threshold braking in a straight line and then turn the steering wheel, the brakes still override and the tire won't generate any lateral force. The key takeaway here is that in both of these situations, there would just be one force line from the tire going directly backwards because the brakes override the steering.

A good way to visualize these braking forces is by filling up part of the traction circle based on how much brake pressure is applied. The more brakes applied, the more the circle is filled up and therefore a greater portion of the side of the traction circle is cut off and can't be used for lateral force. Maximum straight-line braking at the limit of traction would fill up the entire circle. There would be no lateral capacity left.

With our partially filled up circle in this figure, we have a new path the force line will take as steering is increased and we've shown several different force lines showing how the tire force will look as steering is increased. The new force lines will follow the edge created by the brake force. Once the line reaches the edge of the circle, we have hit the traction limit. You can see how this partial amount of braking allows less lateral force than when no braking was applied earlier. As the brakes are increased, you would be able to generate less lateral grip.

This is the front tire we are showing, but the rear tire is also going to be braking and will have its own circle filling up. The brake bias effectively alters the rate the front and rear circles fill up. As long as the bias is set so that the lateral force requirement sent back hits the rear circle inside its current lateral capacity, the car will still understeer. This is why a more rearward brake bias can cause oversteer, as the rear circle would fill up faster than the front and the force sent back is more likely to go outside the rears current lateral capacity.

The way these brake forces will look during a typical corner entry situation is this. The driver would start with full brakes and no turning. The circle would be completely full so there would be only the tiniest of spaces at the bottom and the force line would go directly backwards. Then the driver will ease off the brakes as they use their understeering yaw sensitivity testing to keep the tire at the edge of the circle as they work their way around to pure cornering as they approach the apex.

Remember again though, the traction circle and force line are not just a pretty representation. That line from the center of the tire to the edge is showing where the tire is actually trying to move the car. The combination of the lines from all four tires is the exact direction and amount the car is being pushed. A sensitive driver will be able to notice how much the car is being accelerated in that direction.

THROTTLE **FORCES**

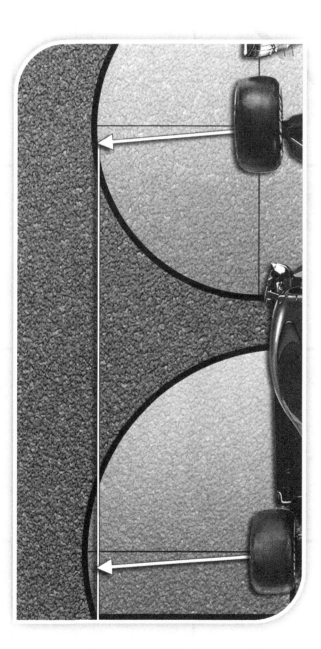

Following steering and brakes, the last of our primary driver inputs is the throttle. Forces from throttle application work much the same way as braking forces. They will override turning forces. A key difference though is that most cars don't have the power to give maximum forward acceleration at race speeds and so the line on the traction circle will rarely, if ever, be pointing straight toward the front. What is more typical is that at full throttle there will always be some turning forces left over and the circle will never be completely filled up.

This illustration shows a car in a typical mid corner scenario where the front tire is sending back some lateral force because the driver is steering left. The driver hasn't applied throttle yet so the rear force line would just be going sideways and slightly backwards from drag to meet the line from the front.

But now we want to apply some power. This illustration shows the most power that can currently be applied without oversteering. The force line at the rear will always go out to try to match the force sent back from the front, but will also always be along the top of the filled throttle area. In this example, the driver has applied as much throttle as they can given the lateral force sent back. We can't fill up the circle with any more throttle because that would make the top of the filled throttle area not reach far enough out to meet the line coming back from the front. This extra throttle would cut off too much of the rear lateral capacity.

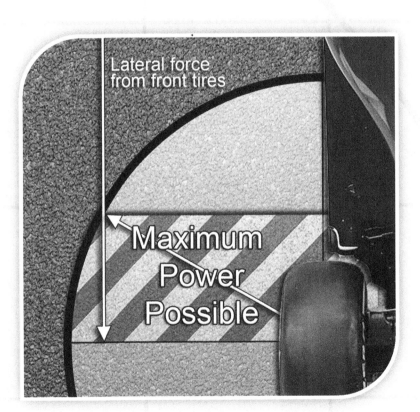

If the driver tried to apply more power, the rear force line would be pushed inward because the throttle overrides the steering. The rear line would then be further inward than the front and the car would begin to oversteer.

To allow extra throttle we must bring the line coming back from the front inward. The way the driver does this is by reducing steering. They can then fill up the rear circle with more power until it hits the new lateral force sent back. The force line is now pointing further forward. Also remember though, the front tire would be pushing to the side and slightly backwards from induced drag counteracting some of that forward force from the back tire. Add all these forces together and you will have the total force pushing on the car.

This tire force section introduces several new concepts and might be somewhat confusing on the first read through. You might consider rereading it if necessary, as we are going to be using these type of illustrations to show how you can manipulate the driver inputs during different phases of the corner to control car balance and movement. This should hopefully all become clearer as we work through specific examples in the upcoming sections.

CAR CONTROL + LINE THEORY

We've now seen how steering, brakes and throttle can affect the direction and magnitude of tire forces. We should also understand from our knowledge of Line Theory that we need to maximize and direct these forces to push us in the ideal direction. So now, we will combine these concepts with our newfound knowledge of car control cues to come up with a unified solution that will allow us to optimize any corner, all from the driver's point of view. We'll see how, although using the Universal Cue will be our final answer to achieving our best performance, there are many other shortcuts we can use to help us along the way.

We're going to break this down into two major sections. Deceleration and acceleration. We generally refer to these as corner entry and corner exit although the acceleration/deceleration phases will also be used in situations that wouldn't fall within the standard definitions of corner entry/exit.

We will then further break the two sections down into understeer and oversteer, as these are the two states you can be in when driving at the limit. We'll learn how a driver can ensure they are right at the limit and producing the maximum tire forces possible while understeering or oversteering. We will also show you how to direct these tire forces optimally while in both states. So here we go, this is what everything we've learned so far has been leading up to.

PART 3 - DECELERATION PHASE
THRESHOLD BRAKING

The deceleration phase doesn't always start with straight line braking, but when it does, the goal is actually fairly simple. Press the brakes as hard as needed to achieve maximum deceleration. While easy to understand, this can actually be one of the hardest to do optimally. The good news is that playing it safe and not going to the very limit of threshold braking is going to have a minimal effect on your lap times. Going too far however, and flatspotting your tires can affect them quite a bit. Understanding what the optimum is and striving toward that should always be kept in mind though, because even small gains are still gains and having great threshold braking skills will also make overtaking and defending overtakes easier.

So how do we accomplish this optimum? Eventually you will want to just use the Universal Cue, but there is a nice well-known shortcut here in that usually maximum deceleration is achieved somewhere just short of tire lockup. If you are in an open wheel car, you can actually see the tires stop moving, but even in closed wheel cars, you can often hear them as well. These are not perfect cues, but they are good enough to get you close for a while as you develop your sensitivity to the Universal Cue.

Maximum deceleration is usually achieved just short of tire lockup.

The Universal Cue will of course be your final answer, and as you improve your corner entry, you will notice an improvement in your threshold braking as well because it's simply a continuation of it. Your overall sensitivity to car movement will improve and you will begin to notice the small changes in deceleration rate right before tire lockup.

Also remember that your initial brake application can be as fast as the load transfer will allow. In general, this is very fast, but you'll need to pay attention to your cues to see how fast this can be. Don't just arbitrarily squeeze your brakes or you are most likely going to be giving up time, but again, you'll never know if you don't pay attention to the proper cues.

There may also be grip variations from track elevation or surface changes, aero forces altering grip with speed, bumps, etc... that can make the grip of the tires vary during the braking zone. By paying attention to the proper cues, a driver can react and modify the needed brake pressure but also, slowly fill in their predictive driving databank for that track and car combo. They will know to expect a bump or change in grip and make the appropriate adjustment.

Remember though that you should never completely preprogram an action and should always be testing the limits. Make sure you don't just get in the habit of pushing the pedal X amount here and Y amount there. We keep bringing this up because it's a natural habit for people to get into. Make sure your driver inputs are always a reaction if possible. Your learned predictions will help you get close, but always be paying attention to your cues and pushing the limits if you wish to improve.

CORNER ENTRY UNDERSTEER

At the point a driver decides to start turning, the straight-line braking portion has ended and we are now in our spiral entry. We are going to start out with looking at corner entry while understeering. We won't even consider the possibility of oversteer. As long as the car is set up for it and the driver doesn't induce oversteer, this is a very real possibility. We'll see later how we generally want to be at the limit of the front tires at corner entry anyway, so this is also an ideal scenario.

To recap from *The Perfect Corner*, we know that during our corner entry, we want to change directions as quickly as possible and we do this by primarily directing our tire forces to push us in the ideal direction. This ideal direction is basically back the way we came at the same angle as the track. Using our knowledge of directing tire forces with different inputs, we can understand why the beginning of the spiral needs primarily braking to create forces pushing us backwards down the track and how you will then need to increase steering while reducing braking to keep that force aimed correctly as you turn through the corner.

Hopefully we can understand this from a physics standpoint, but how can we ensure that we are actually accomplishing this from the driver's point of view? While the option of just doing an arbitrary smooth transition from braking to steering is always there, we should strive for something more specific to guide us. While the final answer can always be to just follow the Universal Cue, let's see if we can tease out some shortcuts.

THE **STEERING WHEEL** SHORTCUT

If you are understeering during corner entry, what to do with your steering wheel is actually pretty easy to understand. You will want to use your understeer sensing ability to keep the car right at the limit of understeer the entire time. Do your testing to see if the car responds by turning more and back off if it doesn't. This should be a constant (ideally automatic) part of your corner entry unless the car goes into oversteer. This is quite a nice shortcut because you don't have to worry about what to do with steering. You will simply keep the front tires as close to the limit as possible, but small mistakes going too far aren't that big a deal at corner entry. If you turn a little too far, it is essentially the same as applying a little bit of extra brakes. This can be compensated for by using a little less actual brakes. A little bit of extra steering hurts much more during corner exit where you ideally don't want to have any braking force at all. We'll look more into that in the corner exit section.

As long as you can keep the steering near the limit, the only thing a driver needs to decide on is the amount of braking to apply. Unfortunately, there are no easy shortcuts to know the amount of braking, but before we look at that a bit more, we wanted to point out one more useful shortcut dealing with steering.

> Whatever braking amount allows the steering wheel to turn faster is correct.

Remember our goal is to change direction as quickly as possible so if we are keeping the steering right at the limit, then the quicker we change direction, the quicker our steering wheel turns. If you have good understeer sensing abilities, you can use this as a shortcut. Whatever braking amount allows the steering wheel to turn faster is correct.

Think about it. Imagine you are at corner entry, have no brakes applied, and then turn the steering wheel until you are right at the understeer limit. This will carry you on a big, circular entry path and you won't be able to turn the steering very quickly as the car is only slowing down from drag forces. On the other end of the spectrum, if you have almost full brakes applied and hold them there you will have very little lateral grip available. You will hit the understeer limit after very little steering and not be able to turn the steering wheel very quickly in that scenario either.

The correct answer of course is a steady reduction in brakes, and whatever amount at any instant that allows the fastest turning of the steering wheel is the correct amount. So therefore, it can be useful to focus on trying to turn the steering as quickly as possible and use whatever braking amount that allows you do that. This is a good, quick way to self-analyze on track as well as check your performance later in telemetry as the steering should always be making a fairly steady increase. Any long pauses without a steering increase or any sudden big increases in steering rate should be looked at.

Be careful with this though. In an effort to turn the steering wheel as quickly as possible, an insensitive driver can blow past the edge of understeer easily so this does require some skill to use effectively. A steady increase in steering angle that is simply a steady increase in the tire sliding and overheating is certainly not the driver's goal.

While paying attention to steering wheel movement can be quite useful, in itself it's generally not enough to achieve the best performance. For one, it requires you to focus some attention on what your steering wheel is doing. Ideally, you'll want to focus on the track by paying attention to how all this affects your car's movement.

THE **EULER SPIRAL** SHORTCUT

In *The Perfect Corner*, we talked a lot about the Euler spiral and how an optimized entry will follow that path. In this way, the Euler spiral is really just a shortcut for the Universal Cue. Again, the Euler spiral is simply the shape of an arc with a constantly decreasing radius. The shape is the result of tire forces being directed correctly. This is quite useful because a good shortcut is to focus on tightening the path we are on as quickly as possible. This is very similar to paying attention to the steering wheel movement, but it's focusing on the track instead of on a cue inside the car.

THE EULER SPIRAL

While trying to turn as quickly as possible however, it's easy to make the mistake of just slowing down too much. This might feel like you are tightening up your radius as quickly as possible, but it would actually be a slower radius reduction. Just like reaching your acceleration point, you want to reduce radius as quickly as possible based on time, not distance. It might be helpful to try to concentrate on maintaining the maximum speed possible while tightening your radius as quickly as possible. Another way to visualize this is by trying the best you can to drive off onto the inside of the track at the apex. If your braking point is late enough, it will be impossible to do so. The ideal braking point while reducing radius as quickly as possible will take you right to the apex.

As you work on this, it can be helpful to intentionally miss the apex. Brake later than you should and then do everything you can to try to get to the apex. If you used your normal braking point and start trying to drive off the inside of the track, you are very likely to actually run off the inside of the track if you start turning faster than normal. By braking later, you give yourself room to tighten up your spiral.

Plus, before you know it, you may surprise yourself and make it to the apex with your new later braking point. This is actually a good way to work up a corner when trying to optimize a new track as well. If you brake late and miss the apex by 10 feet, you simply need to back up your braking point 10 feet. If done properly this is a lot quicker than moving your braking point forward a few feet at a time.

Focusing on tightening your line is quite useful, but eventually you'll want to just go directly to the source, the Universal Cue, so let's now look at how that can be used during corner entry.

THE **UNIVERSAL CUE** DURING **CORNER ENTRY**

> Optimizing your tire force direction will cause the car to turn as quickly as possible, so whatever is reducing your radius faster is always the right answer.

At this point, we aren't really talking about shortcuts anymore, as our eventual goal is to simply pay attention to the car's overall movement on track. We want to be the astronaut aiming our fire extinguisher. All the car control and rotation business will just become automatic and fade away. For a driver that is well trained in the Universal Cue, even the first time they do a corner in a car they've never driven, you could look at telemetry and see the smooth transition from brakes to steering and then maximum acceleration from the apex. It may not be fully optimized yet and will take some time to perfect, but none of their actions were pre-planned or a line they were taught. They were simply the result of trying to maximize the car's movement toward the ideal direction. If you can do that, you will know how to drive anything, anywhere.

To accomplish this, you will need to be able to visualize where you are in relation to the corner as a whole as well as the speed and direction you are moving at any instant. Then as you go through the corner, you use your driver inputs to maximize the total forces pushing the car in the ideal direction. During your braking zone, this will be threshold braking. Then a combination of braking and steering at corner entry. At the apex, it will be pure lateral cornering. Then at corner exit, it will be generating as much acceleration in the ideal direction as possible.

We've talked about the ideal direction a lot, but how can a driver visualize it? The astronaut had his spaceship to focus on getting to, but as a driver, you'll need to imagine it. For corners with a normal straight approach, your ideal direction is quite easy to discern as you will just be at the edge of the track as you approach and your direction is already set by the angle of the track. During something like a complex sequence of corners or an autocross course with cones however, it can be more difficult. In this case, your ideal direction is set by the direction you are traveling as you begin to turn and these type of corners often allow the driver to decide this direction. Unfortunately, this also adds another layer of complexity and another way to make a mistake.

We also want to make sure you understand that you shouldn't actually be looking in the ideal direction. You should be looking at as much of the corner as you can and then doing your best to visualize your path through the corner as if from an overhead view. You are then trying to generate as much total tire force as you can to push you toward the ideal direction throughout the entire corner. It might also be helpful to think back to the cannibal marauders example from *The Perfect Corner*. During corner entry, you could visualize trying to get the car to move away from something as quickly as possible coming from the opposite of the ideal direction. You know that you want to turn the car away as quickly as possible, but once that turning is complete, you want to have as much speed as you can to keep going. Hopefully this might help you not over-slow the car while trying to turn as quickly as possible.

IDEAL DIRECTION

THE **OTHER** DIRECTION

We talk a lot about maximizing forces to push us in the ideal direction, but it can also be useful to pay attention to the "other direction." If you remember from advanced racing physics in *The Perfect Corner*, if our ideal direction was on the X-axis, the Y-axis would be the other direction. The sideways force that we use to move us across the track toward the apex.

Paying attention to this can be useful because if we start to notice we either are accelerating too quickly or have stopped moving along the Y-axis, we know that our primary forces are not maximized as well as they could be. Our movement toward the apex on the Y-axis should have a steady increase in velocity. If our movement becomes too fast, then we need to bring our tire forces toward the back of the car with an increase in braking. If they've slowed or even stopped, we know we need less braking.

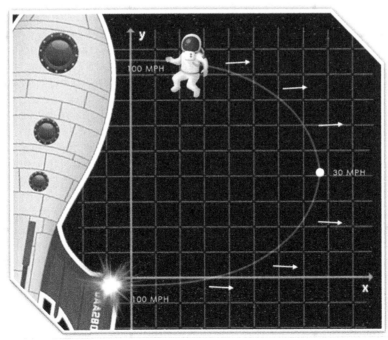

Using the minimum sideways force to arrive at the perfect Y-axis velocity at the apex for an ideal corner exit is the goal.

Also consider that in less than a 180 degree corner, part of your Y-axis velocity becomes your new X-axis velocity after the apex. Let's take a look at how that works now.

PARTIAL-SPIRAL **CORNER ENTRY**

Up to this point, we have only been using the full 90-degree spiral entry as an example. When you have a high angle corner like a 180-degree hairpin, the driver is able to make a steady transition from full brakes to no brakes during corner entry as steering is increased. This gives you the classic, smooth trailing off brakes as you go through the full 90 degrees of the spiral. But what happens when the corner is less angled and doesn't need the full spiral?

Remember, a driver's corner entry goal is always to reduce radius quickly with an ideal direction backwards down the track. Following this, if the driver were trying to move the car in the ideal direction during corner entry in a corner with very little direction change, they would still need to generate force almost completely backwards as they reached the apex. This would require them to still apply significant brake pressure the very instant before they should be going to maximum acceleration at the apex.

Clearly this isn't possible, as you can't instantaneously go from heavy brakes to acceleration. Instead, the driver will need to end their braking earlier than what might be theoretically optimal as this will allow them time to set up for the corner exit properly. This is because maximizing corner exit performance is vital for good lap times.

Corner Entry

81 | P a g e

The effect this has on driver inputs at corner entry is important. The driver will have a typical steady drop off in braking for most of the corner entry that mirrors the full spiral approach, but at some point prior to the apex, the braking force will drop quickly so the driver can set up for acceleration at the apex. This means that **for less than a full 90-degree entry, there absolutely should not be smooth decrease in braking from entry to apex**. The only time you should see a linear decrease in braking is during an entry that goes the full 90 degrees of the spiral. For anything less, there needs to be a faster drop in braking at some point prior to the apex.

How this will look from a force direction standpoint is that the driver will move to a new ideal direction prior to the apex. In other words, at some point in the entry spiral, they will switch to a new spiral that would mimic a 180-degree turn leading into that corner exit. This will let them trail off the brakes all the way at the apex to allow a proper transition to acceleration. This illustration shows how the ideal direction will change as they switch from the original dark spiral to the new white one

The effect this has is that although steering rate won't change much, a driver would have an increased rate of braking reduction at some point to quickly match the new spiral and new ideal direction. The driver would then return to a steady brake reduction as they approach the apex on the new spiral.

All of this happens within one or two seconds at most usually, so often you need to look at telemetry to see what is really going on. If you watch the brake trace of a world-class driver in corners with little direction change needed you usually see a faster brake reduction at some point prior to the apex. For the very best drivers this will be quite close to the apex and then normally only drag forces or very light braking is used to slow down the last little bit prior to the acceleration point.

This may sound complicated with switching spirals and changing force directions and such, but we wanted to explain how it works from a physics standpoint. That way you can understand what you are seeing and realize that the fast reduction in braking during entry to a corner with little direction change needed is not an error. It's absolutely necessary. From the driver's point of view, it should simply feel like you are trying to reduce your radius as fast as possible during corner entry, but giving yourself enough time to set up for the acceleration phase. Because of the physics involved, this requires an increased rate of brake reduction at some point during your entry, not a smooth linear reduction from entry to apex.

The closer you can carry this heavier braking to the apex before switching to the new spiral, the longer you keep your forces pushing you in the ideal direction and thus achieve a lower elapsed time. This is why it is very important to be aware of the shape of the corner because the ideal direction follows the angle of the track. Yet again, this is why it's important to react to cues. A preprogrammed smooth transition from brakes to steering can get you close to the optimum in a 180-degree corner, but in many, it will be giving up time to the more knowledgeable driver.

CORNER ENTRY OVERSTEER

Our corner entry up until now has always been with an understeering car. We haven't had to worry about balance at all, only using the Universal Cue to keep our tire forces pushing us in the ideal direction. In some cars, this will actually happen if they are set up to understeer enough. We actually recommend for drivers to keep their cars heavily biased toward understeer as they develop these basic corner entry skills so they don't have to worry about entry oversteer as it is usually many driver's biggest problem.

At some point however, it will be something every driver will eventually need to worry about. While for optimum corner entry performance you want to use the maximum grip of the front tires, if you are also using as much of the rear tires as possible, you will inevitably go too far sometimes and have to deal with oversteer. A driver's ability to ride the edge of oversteer during corner entry is where the last bit of lap time usually hides.

The reasons for oversteer at corner entry can be plentiful, but the car's setup is the overriding factor of how susceptible it will be. If you bias a car's setup further from understeer, you will be closer to the limit of rear traction so a bump, too much or too little brakes, or too much yaw rate from a fast turn-in can push the rear tires past their limit. Even if driven perfectly though, an optimally setup car will usually always have at least one portion of corner entry that will make it go into oversteer. If it doesn't, then it means the setup is most likely not using all potential grip.

Whatever the reason for the oversteer though, the driver's response is usually going to be the same because oversteer at corner entry is almost never ideal except possibly in certain unique circumstances such as rear-brake karts or off-road racing.

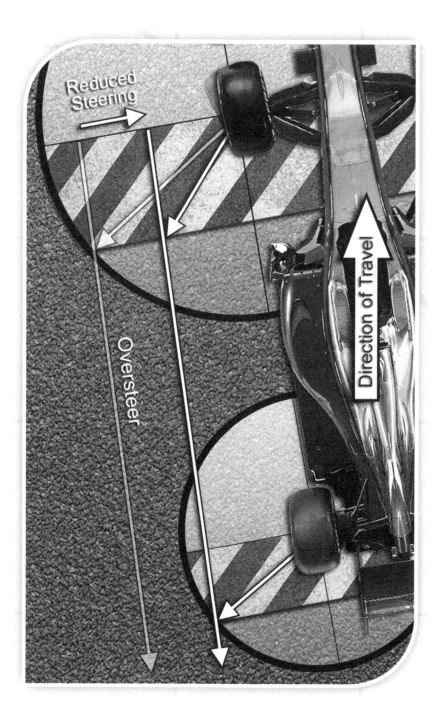

Reduced
Steering

Oversteer

Direction of Travel

For most situations, a driver will want to get out of oversteer as quickly as possible and to do this they need to reduce the lateral force at the front and increase it at the rear. This is primarily going to be with a reduction in steering, but also possibly a change in whatever driver input might have reduced the rear lateral force in the first place.

Let's take a look at the tire forces to see how this works. This illustration shows a car that started to oversteer because the original shaded force line from the front was further out than the line at the rear. This was during corner entry so there was a lot of forward load transfer changing the relative circle sizes from the braking force.

You want to stay in understeer during corner entry, as the more heavily loaded front tires with more capacity will provide the greatest force possible.

Then you will ideally use the rear tires as much as possible to add to the total force acting on the car.

You can see how by reducing the steering, the line at the front will move inwards closer to the car and require less grip from the rear tires. If you look back at the illustration that shows tire forces from steering, you'll see that you could technically also steer even more to hook the line around and bring it closer to the car, but this is generally not your best option.

You can also see how the driver keeps the same level of braking force, but just reduces steering until the force sent back moves inside the available circle left over at the rear tires and the car stops oversteering. But really, we shouldn't say the car is no longer oversteering, just that the driver is now controlling the oversteer. A skilled driver could keep the car in this state by using yaw sensitivity to provide just the right amount of steering needed to keep the rear tires right at the limit.

By our definition however, the car is still technically in oversteer because we cannot achieve understeer. If the driver increased steering again, the car would just start accelerating in yaw again. It's really excessive yaw velocity when the lateral force at the front is bigger than the rear that we are trying to avoid. If the driver let the yaw go really far before correcting, they would need to countersteer and generate force in the complete opposite direction to control the oversteer. If the car started going so far sideways that they would hit the maximum steering lock before generating the needed countersteering force, it would be an unsavable spin. Oversteer to an unsavable angle can happen very quickly sometimes.

Having great yaw sensitivity to detect and fix that first hint of oversteer that only requires a tiny steering correction before a big one is needed requires lots of practice. Rear-brake only karts are terrific for developing this skill. As they only have brakes on the rear wheels, if you want to move those tire forces to push you more rearward in the ideal direction you are also courting oversteer the entire time. Remember, when you only have rear brakes, only the rear tire circles are going to be filling up and cutting off the lateral capacity, unlike 4-wheel brakes where both front and rear are going to be filling up together.

A car with a very forward brake bias can be driven less precisely during entry without fear of spinning. The front circle is always filling up faster so you can't get the lateral force line of the front to go outside the rear unless you use extreme driving techniques such as the Scandinavian Flick.

We also want you to notice that in the oversteer illustration, the reduction in steering to bring that front line closer to the car is showing a reduction in force. The driver is no longer using the front tires to maximum capacity, although they still would be using the rears to the limit. This is why we want to stay in understeer during corner entry, as the more heavily loaded fronts with more capacity will provide the greatest force possible. Then you will ideally use the rears as much as possible to add to the maximum total force. With the car depicted in the oversteer illustration, the rear tires are limiting the total force even if controlled perfectly at the limit. This driver would need to adjust brake bias or other setup parameters to more equally use all four tires and generate greater total force.

There is another solution however, and it's a special braking technique we'll look at shortly. Brakes can have a great influence over our ability to control the car at corner entry so let's look at a few different braking techniques and see how they might fit our goals.

LEFT FOOT VS RIGHT FOOT BRAKING

Each done optimally, there isn't going to be a big difference in lap times between left foot and right foot braking. The transition time moving the foot over from throttle to brake has an almost negligible effect on lap times and the move back to throttle during the transition phase usually shouldn't be as fast as possible anyway. If there were a race coming up soon, we'd recommend a driver should just use whatever foot they are best with.

If you are interested in long-term training and improvement however, we would have to go with left foot braking. The only real negatives are that it makes it harder to use a clutch and if you have been right foot braking your whole life, it can feel as if you are starting over. Given sufficient practice though, left foot braking will open up new car control techniques that right foot braking just cannot compete with.

One problem with left foot braking is that traditionally it can only be done in a car or corner that doesn't require the clutch to downshift. There is however, a little known technique that can rectify this problem called switch-foot braking. With this technique you start with traditional right foot braking as you downshift, but once the shift is completed, you switch your braking foot prior to turn in. This is easier if you have a wide enough brake pedal to momentarily use both feet at once, but if not, quickly switching feet will still work. But what exactly is so great about left foot braking to make all this hassle worth it?

We mentioned that, done optimally, times would be nearly the same for right or left foot braking. Often though, corner entry is anything but optimal and using left foot braking offers an extra way of controlling the car by having your right foot free to do something else. A secret weapon of many top drivers, combining braking with throttle can open up a whole new realm of car control possibilities.

THROTTLE + BRAKING

Popularized by Michael Schumacher and what some people consider akin to witchcraft, combining throttle and braking is a very real technique and done properly affords you control that is otherwise impossible.

When we were discussing corner entry oversteer we mentioned that the way you typically correct is by reducing steering and this is the way you must do it if you only used pure braking. Many world-class drivers can achieve top times with pure braking alone, and it is an absolutely vital technique that every driver should spend time training before even considering mixing braking with throttle. Pure braking is when only brakes are applied without adding in throttle. This can be done with the right **or** left foot.

As we saw when using pure braking though, even driven optimally, if you get corner entry oversteer, the overall car grip will be limited by the rear tires. The fronts are not providing all they can. This makes setting the corner entry balance through brake bias, dampers, differential settings, etc... vital to lap times.

Many times though, a car cannot be setup to have an optimum balance throughout the entire corner. If you set up to optimize for corner exit (which you should) sometimes corner entry balance can be heavily compromised. A good example would be a low-powered car that needed a very loose setup to maximize corner exit. This can create a car that wants to significantly oversteer as you approach the apex. Even if the driver has a high level of skill and the oversteer is controlled perfectly, the overall force produced is still compromised because you are limited by the rear tires.

There is a better option however. If you combine throttle and braking, you can dynamically adjust the brake bias throughout corner entry to keep the car right at the limit of the front **and** rear tires. You are not compromising your tire force amount and direction by having to reduce steering as you would with pure braking. This will allow you to keep just about any car optimally balanced at corner entry even if the setup is not ideal. The way this works is that applying throttle while braking will add a force working against the rear brakes. From a tire force standpoint, this will reduce how much the rear circle is filled up and give it more lateral capacity. The more throttle applied, the emptier the rear circle becomes and the more lateral capacity available to match whatever is being sent back from the front. Ideally you will apply just the right amount of throttle so the rear circle is filled up to exactly the point that the line sent back from the front hits where the braking meets the edge of the circle. This would use both front and rear to maximum capacity.

You could achieve the same effect if you had a cockpit brake bias adjuster and constantly adjusted it during corner entry to control balance. We've never seen anyone do that effectively, but it's against our principles to say it's impossible to do it that way. Mixing throttle and braking is a proven technique though, so we'll recommend using that option.

From the driver's point of view, this will start with trail braking into the corner as usual, but if you start to get oversteer, you will apply enough throttle counteracting the brakes to reduce the rear braking force only. This will eliminate the oversteer while also keeping the front tires right at the edge of understeer. Too little throttle will make the car continue to oversteer and too much will bring the rear tire force line away from the limit and not use the rear to the maximum. This is in contrast with pure braking where you would reduce steering to reduce the front tire forces to avoid the oversteer. The throttle + braking will keep your tire force amounts and directions more optimized because both front and rear tires can stay at the limit instead of just the rears.

If you think this sounds difficult, you would be absolutely right. To have the skill to pay attention to the Universal Cue and keep the left foot at the correct braking pressure while using yaw sensitivity to control balance with throttle is incredibly difficult. Many drivers that first attempt this will simply apply excessive throttle and brakes and simply understeer around the corner. The goal of this technique is to tighten your radius faster, not just use it to make the car understeer excessively. You need to make sure you are using the optimum brake pressure to maximize the front tires while using the minimum throttle necessary to prevent oversteer. A driver skilled at this can actually use their feet to modify the yaw of the car in the corner. They are constantly testing with using less throttle to see if it increases their turning rate or makes the car go into oversteer.

This is a great technique and we wanted to discuss it, but it definitely fits into the advanced driver category. You should have a really good skill base and be quite competent driving with more traditional techniques before attempting this.

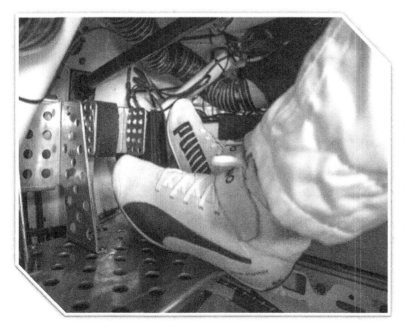

Proper racing shoes as well as adequate cockpit heel and leg support offer greater precision when operating the pedals.

ENGINE BRAKING

This is also a good time to talk about engine braking and its effect on car control. Engine braking is created by the vacuum in the engine that acts as a braking force on the driven wheels anytime the throttle is not applied.

The lower the gear or the higher the rpm at the point the throttle is released, the greater the braking force. The amount of force will vary depending on the car as well, and in some, it can be very significant. Just drop the throttle while you drive to test how much sudden deceleration you get. Also notice how the force will change in different gears and at different rpm.

In a rear-wheel drive car, this braking force will fill up some of the rear circle anytime there is no throttle applied and cut off some of the lateral capacity. During straight-line braking, this can be compensated for by adjusting brake bias, but when a driver turns and begins trail braking, the force from the brakes will reduce, but the engine braking will remain. This will effectively alter the brake bias throughout corner entry. A limited slip differential with some locking under deceleration can counteract this, but an open differential car will tend to go toward oversteer.

This is one further way that throttle + braking can be effective as you can dynamically control this amount of engine braking and therefore brake balance. Engine braking can be an issue during corner exit as well however. If a car begins to oversteer under power, it will often be a driver's instinct to release the throttle. This immediately adds engine braking which not only cuts off some lateral capacity at the rear, but the braking force transfers load to the front adding grip there while removing it from the rear. Since the car had already started to oversteer, unless the driver does some significant countersteering to remove a lot of front tire force there is a high probability of a spin.

If you have significant oversteer under power and a reduction in steering is not sufficient to correct, the ideal solution is to release throttle to what is often called neutral throttle. This is a certain minimal amount of throttle that not only removes engine braking, but also counteracts any induced drag force on the rear tires. It provides the maximum lateral capacity the rear tires can provide to save the spin.

We'll go over power oversteer in depth in a bit, but wanted to go ahead and point out the role engine braking plays before moving on.

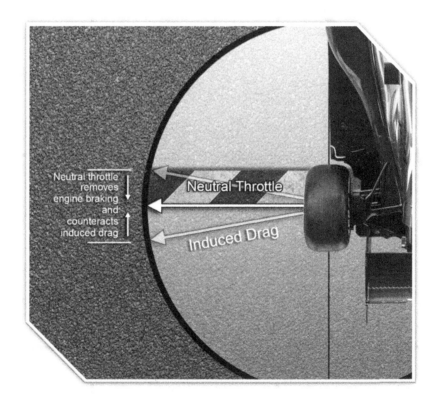

THE **TRANSITION**

The transition phase begins when we are no longer focused on decelerating and are now thinking about accelerating. Although this is typically when you are moving from corner entry to exit, anytime you go from deceleration to acceleration or back again, we call it a transition. This could be in the middle of a chicane or during a correction for example.

> We want to minimize the time of transition, but we also must maintain maximum tire force production as we go through it.

The interesting thing about the transition phase is that ideally we don't even want one. If you go back to the astronaut section from *The Perfect Corner*, you will see that there is almost no transition phase at all in a 180-degree turn, and in the 90-degree turn, the transition phase would only be the quick change in direction of the extinguisher as the astronaut passes the apex. The faster he can aim his extinguisher in the new direction the better. The same is true for a car.

We want to minimize the time of transition, but we also must maintain maximum tire force production as we go through it. These conflicting goals can make things difficult because we are dealing with lots of variables during the transition. One of the most noticeable is that the yaw is changing from an increase in rotation rate to a decrease. As we learned about in the section on yaw inertia, cars resist this change and want to continue turning at the same rate so they have a tendency to go into oversteer as you transition. Again, this is how a Scandinavian flick works. You start a quick rotation in one direction and use that to create oversteer in the opposite. This is usually only beneficial in off-road racing though. In asphalt racing, having oversteer at the apex is typically a problem because in order to transition to acceleration we must have at least some rear tire capacity left over.

The other important aspect of the transition phase is that we want to maintain maximum grip (force) as we move from deceleration to acceleration. You might want to think of this as needing to move the load "around the car" from the front, to the outside, and then to the rear. This is usually not a problem during corners with a lot of direction change like a hairpin where we have trailed off the brakes all the way to pure cornering. But if it's a straighter, high-speed corner where we have cut off a good bit of the end of the Euler spiral, there would be a significant ideal direction change at the apex. The theoretical optimum would have you transferring heavy loads from the front to the back of the car instantaneously.

This is clearly impossible, so in order to maintain maximum overall tire grip as you transition, you will need to compromise your tire force direction for a little bit by switching to the new spiral early as we talked about it in the partial-spiral corner entry section. The straighter the corner and the more of the spiral we cut off, the greater the compromise will most likely need to be. As we near the apex, this will cause our tire forces to momentarily be pushing us in a less than ideal direction more toward the inside of the corner and our rate of radius reduction will be reduced. For most cars and drivers however, this creates less of a time penalty than if we tried to go straight from heavy braking to acceleration, but weren't using the full grip of the tires as we went between them. Only a perfectly driven car that transferred load instantaneously would be able to do the theoretical optimum.

WHEN TO **TRANSITION**

So how do we know when to end our deceleration and begin this transition to acceleration? How long should we let these compromised tire forces last? This primarily comes down to how long the driver thinks they need to set up the car to be ready to go to throttle. Another way to think of this is that it's when the driver changes their focus from tightening their radius to finding their ideal throttle application point.

> As soon as a driver realizes that going to throttle will take them to the edge of the track at corner exit their acceleration phase has begun.

Because corner exit performance has the greatest effect on lap times, a driver needs to move their focus as early as necessary to ensure they do the corner exit properly. If you have a picture perfect Euler spiral entry, but apexed too late and were 10 mph too slow at the apex, your lap times will suffer significantly. This could even mean losing a few seconds if there is a significant straightaway afterwards. In comparison, if you do a traditional circular entry with less than ideal tire force direction, but your apex allowed you an optimal corner exit, the lap time penalty would most likely be a few tenths of a second at most.

Because of this corner exit importance, for a more novice driver, the transition phase might even need to be the entire corner entry. They might need to focus all their attention on getting the proper apex and corner exit and not even worry about trying to tighten their corner entry radius. As soon as a driver realizes that going to throttle will take them to the edge of the track at corner exit, their acceleration phase has begun. This could be well prior to the apex if they started braking too early or it could be out in the middle of the track if they missed their apex. But if they didn't realize how off they were until they reached their standard apex, by that time it's too late. A mistake that might have only cost them a few 10ths now might cost them a few seconds. Even a very skilled driver may need to have a longer transition phase in difficult high-speed corners though. We talked about turn 6 at Laguna Seca in *The Perfect Corner* as an example of this. Turn 6 is a very high-speed corner and the total direction change needed is only around 45 degrees. This means you would only be using the very beginning of the spiral and you would theoretically want to still carry significant braking right as you reach the apex. You don't have the longer period of time and steady brake reduction a 180-degree corner affords you.

Full throttle ends

Many cars in this corner would ideally even need to turn in at full throttle and then go to brakes and then back to full throttle all within less than a second. The risk of over-slowing and ruining your corner exit or just totally losing control is high. It might be advisable to set up your exit early and do more coasting or light braking as you approach the apex. This will allow you to give more focus on predicting when you can go to throttle to maximize corner exit. The lap time penalty for doing it this way is quite small whereas the risk of trying to decelerate all the way to the apex for minimal gains is quite high.

Remember though, Line Theory teaches us there is not a corner in the world that you shouldn't decelerate all the way to the apex, but sometimes only the very best drivers can do this successfully and consistently. Just make sure that if you choose to compromise your entry and have a longer transition phase you are doing it on purpose and realizing that you are losing possible time. In training sessions, pushing your skills further to be able to consistently find that last little bit is what we all should strive for. In a race situation however, corner exit optimization is so vital to lap times that understanding your limitations and playing it safe might be ideal.

DRIVER **PREDICTIONS** & FIXING **MISTAKES**

As we've learned, from a lap time perspective, a driver's ability to predict exactly when and where the throttle can be applied to maximize corner exit is all-important. We say, **predict**, because really that is all it is, a prediction. An (educated) guess. The first time even a world-class driver takes a car through a corner and goes to throttle, they might only have a vague idea where their acceleration arc will take them. Even in a car they are familiar with, but in a new corner, they could be very wrong about where their arc will take them. Weather, different bankings, elevation changes, and type of surface can have a significant effect.

If a driver arrives at the apex at the wrong angle and speed, there is absolutely nothing they can do to totally fix it at corner exit and they will be giving up time. They can only do the best with what they have and take mental notes for the next lap. Improving your predictive driving is all about paying attention to how your guess paid off at corner exit and modifying your corner entry and apex to bring you closer and closer to an optimal solution. A driver is predicting a braking point, then predicting a spiral start point and speed, and then finally predicting an apex. All the while using their reactive driving skills to ideally fix any mistakes or bad predictions, while also updating their predictions for the next lap.

This idea of fixing mistakes is very important because really that is all a driver is doing constantly in a corner. They make a prediction and then fix the mistakes. Making mistakes is actually required to drive at the limit. Ideally, these mistakes are very small, but technically that is what they are. As an example, when a driver is doing their steering wheel movements to test for and find the limit of the tires, they are basically just constantly correcting mistakes. Turn the steering more, nope that didn't turn the car more, better back off quickly because we are increasing drag. That was a mistake. An absolutely necessary mistake to let the driver know they were at the limit already. If they had not made it, they would have no way of knowing for sure if they were at the limit of the tires or not. Remember, even a tire testing machine would require at least some movement and testing to keep a tire at peak grip.

The same principle of constantly fixing mistakes is also true for Line Theory. If you find your prediction was bad and your current path is not ideal, you simply re-evaluate your current situation using Line Theory principles. Did you start your spiral going too slow and are going to head off the inside of the track? Re-evaluate the current situation as if you are starting from your current point and speed. You would set a new spiral and apex. What if you missed your braking point and won't make the apex? You re-evaluate and your new ideal apex is now out in the middle of the track. What if you got on the throttle too early and are heading off track at corner exit? You re-evaluate from your current situation. In this case, you would technically need to transition back to the deceleration phase for a split second and then transition to the acceleration phase again.

During all these mistakes and corrections, you obviously aren't really stopping and sitting there to re-evaluate though. It should be an automatic, constant process. This is why having an intuitive understanding of Line Theory is so important because you are doing this constant re-evaluation the entire way through a corner. Always. If you are driving reactively, as we've learned you should, you will never stop making small modifications to your spiral, apex, etc...

You want to make that small correction early and quickly, before you need a big correction that costs you lots of time. In this way, every single driver input is making or correcting a mistake and technically the best drivers make the most. Reactive driving is all about making and fixing mistakes. The more you are able to correct, the better. If you have a top driver with excellent car control skills, a commentator might remark how they were driving flawlessly, but the driver would know they made about a thousand mistakes in their last lap alone.

PART 4 - ACCELERATION PHASE

Although the corner exit acceleration phase is most important from a lap time perspective, it's also where a car shows its greatest limitations. Corner entry and finding the proper apex are all about dealing with those limitations. During the entire corner entry, most cars can use all four tires to the maximum if the driver has the skill. That is why almost all cars can achieve very similar Euler spiral shaped paths while trail braking. But once we hit the acceleration phase, the ideal path different cars take starts to differ widely. We will have variations in the cars' acceleration arcs based on their turning vs acceleration capabilities. Another difference from corner entry is that while we ideally always want understeer at corner entry by using the limits of the front tires, during corner exit, we will have some cars that will understeer and some that will oversteer. This will require different approaches. To tackle this we are going to start off with the easiest and most common corner exit situation and work our way toward the more difficult.

LOWER-POWERED CAR ARC
PERFECT EULER SPIRAL ARC
DRAG RACING CAR ARC

Ideal acceleration arcs will vary depending on a car's lateral vs propulsive force generating capabilities.

FULL THROTTLE **CORNER EXIT**

Most low-powered racecars should be at full throttle from the apex out for most corners on a racetrack. If the corner is fast enough however, even very powerful cars should be at full throttle. This is the most common corner exit and the easiest to figure out because it also has a great shortcut we'll go over.

First things first though, let's take a look at how our tire forces look in this type of corner exit so we can understand what's going on from a physics standpoint. Here is an illustration of a car that has just reached the apex and is about to go to throttle. You can see that we are understeering because the front tires are at the limit of lateral grip and the rear tires are just shy of that because they have a little bit of capacity left over after they match the lateral force sent back from the front.

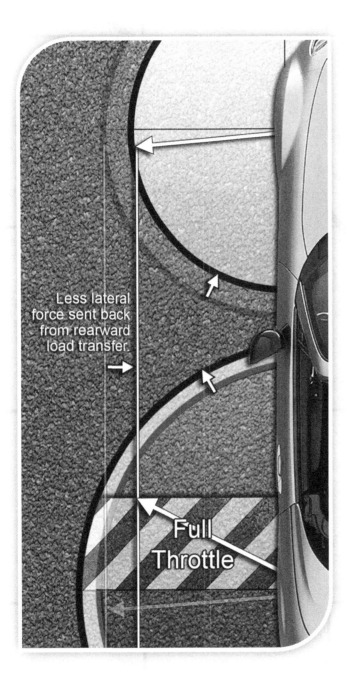

Less lateral
force sent back
from rearward
load transfer.

Full
Throttle

In this next illustration, we've added a new force line from the rear tire to show how the forces move as the driver goes to full throttle. You can see how the rear tire force line moves toward the front of the car, but is still a good bit inside the new larger rear circle so the car would most definitely still be understeering.

What is happening here is that the throttle application and acceleration shifts load to the rear so the rear circle would grow and the front circle would shrink. This causes a reduction in lateral force sent from the front and also greater potential grip at the rear.

Remember, the rear tires can't supply any greater amount of lateral force than is sent back from the front and being at full throttle, this is the most you are going to get out of this car unless you alter the setup.

This shift in load and therefore balance is nonlinear in nature, but is fairly proportional at lower acceleration levels. Because of this, it actually takes a good amount of power to actually create oversteer in a car at corner exit unless the driver was already carrying oversteer to the apex.

This last part is very important. Even a very low-powered car can have "power oversteer" if the driver is over the limit of the rear tires at the apex. In order to achieve this load transfer that shifts relative grip to the rear, the car needs to be able to begin accelerating and needs at least some rear tire capacity left over to do that. Remember, load transfer is from actually achieving acceleration, not just adding throttle. If you are already oversteering, adding throttle normally just makes it worse.

During corner entry, if you have a little bit of oversteer, it is not too terrible as the tire forces will still be pushing you close to the ideal direction. But if you are still oversteering as you reach the apex and try to apply throttle, it just won't work because there is no grip left over to accelerate. You would get rear wheelspin and the car would just oversteer even more. This is not true power oversteer yet though, it would just be considered induced oversteer. Unfortunately, it can also sometimes be hard for new drivers to detect whether they are truly oversteering and are past the grip peak at the apex or just have some sideways yaw from slip angle, but still have a little rear capacity left over.

A way for a driver to learn the difference between true power oversteer and induced oversteer can be done on a skidpad or a long corner. You will simply bring the car to steady state understeer and then increase throttle. You might be surprised how hard it is to get oversteer in this situation, but if you do, it would be true power oversteer. If you have to give the steering a flick (creating excess rotation rate) while applying throttle to initiate oversteer, then you have induced oversteer.

Back to our tire forces though, assuming you are able to apply throttle successfully, let's move forward to late in the corner exit. We can see in this illustration how even at full power our rear tires forces are pushing us very far inward away from the ideal direction. The front tires forces are doing even worse however, and are almost totally sideways from the ideal direction.

So what's going on here? I thought we wanted to get our tire forces pushing us down the track. Yes, we absolutely do, but unfortunately, in this car, this is the best we are going to get. While the tire forces right now don't look so good, the **total net force** pushing us down the track during the entire corner exit is the highest possible. This is why slower cars have a more circular corner exit as this keeps the total forces pushing them in the ideal direction better through the entire corner exit.

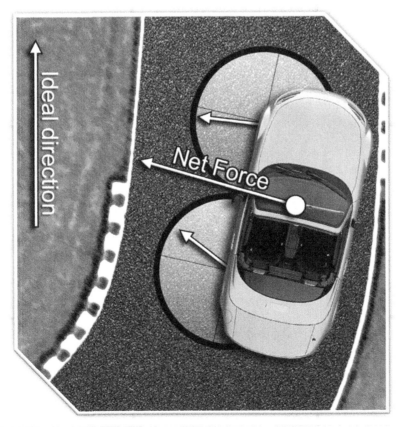

As we introduced in *The Perfect Corner*, almost all cars actually accelerate in the ideal direction better early in the corner exit when they are more sideways to the final direction of travel than when close to going straight at the end. This is a hard concept for many drivers to wrap their head around so we have further examples coming up soon.

For a driver, the car control implications of this more circular exit are quite important. While they simply need to keep the throttle flat to the floor, using the steering wheel properly to maximize front tire lateral grip while minimizing induced drag can create significant lap time gains or losses. Remember how as the steering turns more and more, the front tire forces head more rearward. Therefore, the driver will want to bring the front tires right to the edge of the traction circle, but turning the steering wheel any further is basically going to be like using brakes.

A driver's yaw sensitivity detecting the rotation rate comes into play here. A driver can detect that the rotation rate of the car slows and then stops increasing right as the front tires reach the limit. Any increase in steering beyond this will not increase the turning rate. This is very important, because any extra steering is just adding drag without increasing lateral force. That extra steering is pushing your net tire force direction further and further from the ideal and an insensitive driver can create significant lap time penalties without realizing it by steering too much.

Therefore, developing this understeer sensitivity is crucial to full throttle corner exit performance. A driver might want to just play it safe and stay short of the limit by smoothly unwinding, but this requires a slower than ideal apex. Also, since the following straightaway speeds will be fairly close either way, a driver might not realize they are losing time. Ideally, you'll want to continue pushing for an earlier and faster apex that will require maximum steering at the limit to stay on track, but **no more.**

Be careful here though. It's very easy to make the mistake of turning the steering a little too much and feel like you did it correctly because that little bit of extra drag slowed you down enough to make the corner. You're actually losing time however and the **only** way to know why is following your car control cues.

A sensitive driver might even use this understeer detection during a race situation where they might need to be in a tire saving mode and ultimate lap times are not the current goal. A skilled driver can detect the slowing of rotation rate as the tire enters the transitional area of grip. They can back off as the rotation rate slows rather than going until the rotation rate completely stops increasing. This allows them to stay on the lower side of the grip peak and be very close to the limit while also preserving their tires as much as possible.

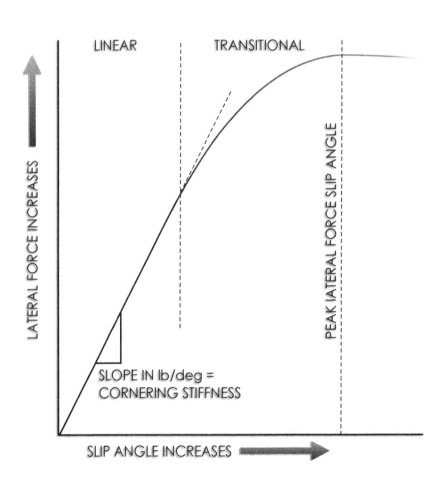

THE **FULL THROTTLE EXIT** SHORTCUT

This last section actually explained the shortcut for a full throttle corner exit. If your car can go to full throttle at the apex without oversteering and you can keep the front tires right at the understeer limit, but just barely stay on track at corner exit then you did it right. Because we are at full throttle, we actually only have one driver input we need to worry about, steering, and why the shortcut works so well. You just have to keep the car as close to the edge of understeer as you can and then adjust your apex accordingly. Being able to apply full throttle is easy, but as you develop your yaw sensitivity, you will become better able to keep the front tires right at the limit without adding excessive drag.

> If you are ever understeering during corner exit, you should also be at full throttle.

Remember, a shortcut allows you a way to figure out how to drive a corner without needing the Universal Cue. In this case, you can just use your understeer sensing abilities to determine the proper corner exit and therefore apex. But of course, a driver can also use the Universal Cue to optimize a full throttle corner exit. As the steering is turned too far and causes extra drag, the movement toward the ideal direction will be slowed. Too little steering will also cause this movement to be slowed however. Only the perfect amount of steering with the perfect apex maximizes the total net force and therefore movement in the ideal direction. Eventually, it should actually be this that a driver is primarily paying attention to. Because not only does it directly follow the physics of racing, but also sometimes, it's all you have.

CORNER EXIT MISCONCEPTIONS

In this last section, the shortcut works because again, a car is either always limited by the front or rear tires. We also know that the more throttle we can use, the more idealized our tire force directions are at corner exit. We can combine these two principles to determine that if you are ever understeering during corner exit, you should also be at full throttle. You should **never** lift to reduce understeer because this also reduces the maximum force you can produce.

You should keep the front tires at the limit by reducing steering if necessary, but never by reducing throttle. If you have to lift in an understeering car, it is **only** because your path would take you off track. You then mentally catalog this as a mistake and use a later apex next time. The only reason you shouldn't use full throttle during corner exit is if you are in a car that can create true power oversteer. We'll look at this near the end of the book.

A similar misconception is the idea of "rotating" a car. There are probably many definitions of what people consider rotating a car, but we are referring to intentionally compromising rear grip to increase yaw. Let's say we have a car that understeers pretty severely during corner exit and what a driver thinks should be their apex would carry them off track if they used full throttle from there. They might complain that the car understeers like a pig. We've now learned that simply means that the driver needs to apex later or ideally adjust their setup, but some drivers may attempt to "rotate" the car. This means they have induced oversteer at the apex so the car's natural tendency to understeer is reduced. They then go to throttle and ride the rear tires on the other side of the grip peak throughout corner exit.

To an unknowing driver this might feel fast. They will be at a higher slip angle and the engine will rev faster (from wheelspin). This would allow them to make the corner from what they think should be their apex as well. Of course, we know that while this may be a fun and visually impressive way to corner, it's not the fastest because your cornering speed is always limited by the front or rear tires. If your car naturally understeers during corner exit, your maximum cornering speed will always be limited by the front tires and short of adjusting your setup there is nothing a driver can do that will improve cornering performance. Don't compromise your rear grip by over-rotating the car just to make it feel more neutrally balanced. While it might subjectively feel better and more balanced to drive, that is only because you have unnecessarily added heat and wear while reducing the force produced from the rear tires.

We want to make it clear however, that it can be fairly easy to fall into this trap of overdriving because it "feels faster," so how are you supposed to know the difference? While you can use yaw sensitivity to control the balance of the car and with enough skill do whatever you want with the slip angle, the only way to really know what balance creates the most acceleration in the ideal direction is the Universal Cue. Put another way, yaw sensitivity gives you the ability to control the car, but the Universal Cue allows you to use that control to reduce your lap times.

In this last example, the driver that "rotated" their car would really have no way of knowing that what they did was slower if they only paid attention to car balance by trying to keep the car at a slip angle they thought "felt good." Sometimes a car has just the right amount of power that full throttle will keep the car in a mild drift at corner exit that looks great and might "feel" fast, but if the driver were sensitive to the Universal Cue, they would notice that this actually reduced their acceleration in the ideal direction, not increased it.

This is quite important because a driver can develop great car control and learn to keep a vehicle stable at virtually any slip angle, but if they aren't able to see how these changes in yaw are affecting the car's movement in the corner, their lap times will be compromised. They may never spin out, but they will be slower than they could be and not know why.

Anytime you are mixing two driver inputs, you must primarily pay attention to the Universal Cue.

This overdriving issue is primarily going to be a problem during corner entry or in a higher-powered car at corner exit because as you move further and further away from just steering at the limit, yaw sensitivity becomes less and less useful as a shortcut. The reason the shortcut cue we use for the full throttle corner exit works so well is that when you are power limited, the corner exit acts just as if you are driving in pure cornering mode like on a skid pad. Just using yaw sensitivity alone to keep the car at the edge of understeer will give you your ideal acceleration arc.

During cornering situations where you are balancing brakes or throttle with steering however, you must primarily use the Universal Cue. To understand why, let's look at an example of a car during a trailbraking corner entry. In general, a car will start with maximum slip ratio and no slip angle during the threshold-braking portion and then will move to the maximum slip angle during pure cornering at the apex. But during the trailbraking portion, the slip angle will generally be increasing and the slip ratio decreasing as the car goes through the spiral.

This can create some confusion as to how a driver should balance brakes and steering if they are only paying attention to yaw sensitivity. At any time during trailbraking, the driver could reduce braking and increase steering and the car would go to a higher slip angle. Alternatively, they could increase brakes and reduce steering and go toward a lower slip angle. In both of these situations, they are still right at the peak of grip though. Having great car control allows them to do this, but how are they supposed to know which combination is best at any instant?

Some drivers might try to get the car to its maximum slip angle with only lateral cornering quickly. To get the car to "take a set." This might feel fast, but the tire forces would be going sideways toward the inside of the corner and this will create a more circular entry path. We've learned that even controlled perfectly at the limit, this will be slower than a spiral entry. You should only reach your maximum slip angle when the ideal direction is directly sideways from you, which is typically only at the apex. In general, there should be a steady increase in slip angle and steering as the slip ratio and braking decrease, but the only way to truly know what driver inputs are needed at any instant is with the Universal Cue. Whatever combination moves the car in the ideal direction the best is correct.

The key here is that anytime you are mixing two driver inputs you must pay attention to the Universal Cue. The corner exit shortcut we went over only works because we are at full throttle and only have to worry about steering. It's just one input. But corner entry blends steering and brakes so it's not quite so easy to figure out what to do. Luckily, corner entry has the Euler spiral, which in itself is a shortcut. But now, we are about to venture into car control situations where there are no shortcuts. The Universal Cue is all you have left and this is perfectly exemplified by high-horsepower, front-wheel drive cars.

THE PROBLEM WITH **FRONT-WHEEL DRIVE**

While front-wheel drive cars are actually quite tame to drive from a car control standpoint as they will rarely spin out, they can be very frustrating when trying to figure out how you should use their capabilities during corner exit.

When a car is front-wheel drive and has enough power to generate wheelspin, at any point you can tradeoff steering and acceleration at will. 4-wheel drive cars can create similar issues, especially in low grip off-road situations, but for now, we'll focus on front-wheel drive only because it's basically a worst-case scenario.

With front-wheel drive, since the power and steering are both supplied by the same tires, the driver can choose how they want to use those tires at any instant. During corner exit, they can increase throttle and reduce steering and create greater forward acceleration. Alternatively, they can use more steering and use less throttle and have more lateral acceleration. This would create two totally different acceleration arcs. Any number of different arcs are possible all while keeping the front tires right at the limit. Because of this, there is not really any easy way to pick which one is best. Again, the reason is that now we have two driver inputs instead of just one that we have to deal with.

Everything we do up until the apex is set up to put the car in the ideal situation to maximize its potential at corner exit. So with the powerful front-wheel drive car, should we do a later apex and bias our corner exit more toward acceleration or do an earlier apex and bias it more toward cornering? Back in *The Perfect Corner*, we mentioned you should go to maximum acceleration as quickly as possible at corner exit. While this is true, maximum acceleration doesn't always mean maximum forward acceleration. If the driver concentrated on just getting on the throttle as quickly as possible in this car, they would need a very late apex and an acceleration arc with a very quickly expanding radius. If they drove perfectly at the limit the entire time and also had all their tire forces going in the proper direction the entire time, they would probably think this is a pretty good approach. They would be slower than ideal however, and would be losing time. So what's the problem here?

While during corner entry, following the Universal Cue will **tighten** the radius as quickly as possible, during corner exit we don't want to **widen** it as quickly as possible. The reason is that tightening the radius quickly is actually just a side effect of having the tire forces going in the proper direction at corner entry. It just gives us a nice shortcut. During corner exit however, although following the Universal Cue will give us an expanding radius, we can always just expand the radius faster by unwinding the steering faster. Because of this, paying attention to how our radius is changing at corner exit is not going to help any, so unless we can find a nice shortcut cue as we have for the low-powered car, all we have to go on is paying attention to our overall movement in the ideal direction.

We only care about the acceleration we can generate toward the ideal direction.

So let's see how we might do this better. When we looked at different acceleration arcs, we learned how lower-powered cars typically have more circular exits and powerful cars have more spiral shaped ones. Our powerful front-wheel drive car, even though it has high horsepower, would actually have a very circular ideal acceleration arc because it has such limited forward acceleration potential. For those unfamiliar, front-wheel drive cars typically have less than ideal acceleration performance from the load transfer off the front tires under power. So even a very powerful, but front-wheel drive car is going to have cornering forces significantly higher than its acceleration forces. It **could** drive a more spiral shaped acceleration arc at the limit of traction, but this would be less than ideal because the total net tire forces would be lower during the exit.

These illustrations show how with the two different exit lines, the car is actually accelerated down the track faster in the middle of the corner exit with a more circular arc. At the end of the corner exit, the cars would both be going straight and will be generating the same force there, but the **total net** corner exit force is greater with the more circular exit. Because of the faster, earlier apex, we get a little increase in (lateral) **acceleration** at the apex, but in the middle of the corner exit, there is going to be the biggest difference.

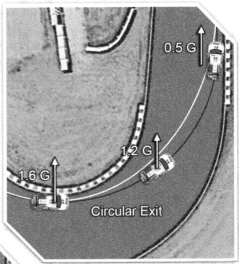

Circular Exit

Again, **we only care about the acceleration we can generate toward the ideal direction**. So what this shows us is that we truly do want maximum acceleration from the apex, but that doesn't necessarily mean forward acceleration from using more throttle. Sometimes that means more lateral acceleration from cornering.

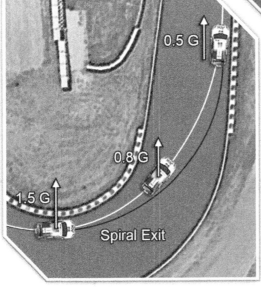

Spiral Exit

You can probably understand how this could cause confusion for a driver. They will actually have better lap times if they apex earlier and use a more circular corner exit with a slower throttle application. If they don't know this, and aren't paying attention to the Universal Cue, even driving perfectly at the limit, they can be beaten by drivers that look like they are driving a slower line, but are actually faster.

Other than just repeated trial and error of every corner, the **only** way a driver will determine the optimum in this car is to follow the Universal Cue. They will need to pay very close attention to how their different apexes and inputs change their acceleration in the ideal direction. They will have to be able to notice that they are actually moving quicker down the track when they are more angled than when they are straighter to their final direction of travel. This actually makes this type of car great for training the Universal Cue as following that is the only way to know how optimum your corner exit is. There are no shortcuts.

When rules allow, front-wheel drive drag cars often use wheelie bars not to prevent wheelies, but to help maintain front tire load under acceleration.

HIGH POWERED **REAR-WHEEL DRIVE**

Front-wheel drive is somewhat rare in racing, but we wanted to cover it because it can teach a lot about your true goal of generating the maximum net tire forces at corner exit.

Let's now go back to a more typical rear-wheel drive setup as we move on to our last type of corner exit where you have enough power that a full throttle exit is no longer possible. While this typically requires a high-powered car, it could also even be a modestly powered car with a forward weight bias, very poor tires, or a wet track. You can actually run into this situation with just about any car with a loose enough setup so let's take minute and talk about that.

Car setup is a huge topic and we aren't going to get into the specific details here; we are only going to discuss the overall goal. While there are lots of books and resources out there on how every setup adjustment works, rarely will you find what the ultimate goal is with those adjustments.

The reason is that in order to understand your true goal with setup you have to first understand Line Theory. Like everything else, the ideal setup is one which allows you to maximize the forces pushing you in the ideal direction. Actually, the goal with just about every setup option is in pursuit of this. Adjusting the ride height, springs, and dampers to handle the curbs better, changing gear ratios, adjusting balance and aero settings are all about maximizing the total net force.

While it might be a good idea in the beginning to setup a car such that it always understeers at the limit and is comfortable to drive, you should understand that this often means a setup that is compromised from a lap time perspective. A more understeering setup may produce more consistent lap times for a more novice skill level, but a more neutral (and harder to drive) setup will use the car's capabilities better.

This is because corner exit introduces the biggest limitations of a car and also makes the biggest lap time difference, so a setup should ideally be focused on best dealing with those limitations. During corner entry, a driver with sufficient skill can typically drive at the limit while optimizing tire force direction even if the setup is focused on the corner exit. They can independently control corner entry balance with brake bias and a few other settings, so an ideal Euler spiral shaped entry is almost always attainable. Corner exit performance however, is going to be much more limited by setup.

> Regardless of setup, an ideal Euler spiral entry is almost always attainable if the driver has the skill.

Let's use our full throttle corner exit car as an example. When you have a car that understeers during corner exit, you are limited by your front tires. At maximum throttle, you won't be using the rear tires to their limit, although you might be very close. If you begin to adjust your setup away from understeer, at some point, you will begin to oversteer under full power. When the setup keeps the car right on a perfect balance at the edge of understeer and oversteer during corner exit then you have found the ideal. This will provide the maximum net tire forces pushing the car toward the ideal direction during corner exit.

In practice, this will very rarely happen and as mentioned earlier would be a transient state at best, but it can give a driver a goal with their setup. Generally, the best that will happen is that in some portions of a corner, the car will understeer and in some, it will oversteer. An important takeaway here is that you still aren't at the point of true power oversteer yet where you will need to lift. When you first start to get oversteer at full throttle you will want to first reduce the steering to bring the front tires lateral force line inward to what the rears can provide. If you continued to try to keep the front tires at the limit, the car would continue oversteering and you would spin.

Again, this is not yet what we consider true power oversteer that requires a throttle reduction. Remember, from a physics perspective, reducing steering moves the front tire force line closer to the car. To prevent oversteer, you need to reduce the front lateral force to what the rear is capable of. This means the front is no longer at the limit, but the rear still will be if you are at full throttle and can keep it right at the limit of controlled oversteer.

**Check out our *STEP-BY-STEP RACECAR SETUP GUIDE*
at paradigmshiftracing.com**

You can use this to guide your setup process. If you always have to reduce steering to prevent oversteer in a certain section you can bias your setup toward greater understeer and will be faster in **that particular section.** This will cause you to be slower in sections where you are still understeering however.

From this, we can gather that under full throttle your corner exit potential is completely controlled by your setup. If you are always understeering, you can loosen your setup and if you always oversteer, you will tighten your setup until you get a little bit of both depending on the exact circumstances. Maximum net force is achieved when you can use full throttle and stay right at the edge of both.

You will find that in general the more power a car has, the more biased toward understeer the car will need to be to maximize total force at corner exit. Conversely, a low-powered car, especially with a rearward weight bias, will need a very loose setup to maximize corner exit, as it will be very unlikely to oversteer under power. Off throttle though, this type of setup will be very prone to oversteer and can make corner entry and achieving the little bit of understeer needed at the apex quite tricky.

But what happens when you get to the point that a setup change or steering reduction is not preventing oversteer at corner exit? What if we must lift to prevent a spin? In that case, we know we have a true power oversteer situation and we need to start deciding how to balance our steering and throttle just like with the powerful front-wheel drive car.

TRUE **POWER** OVERSTEER

Just like how we said a full throttle corner exit is achievable in virtually any car in a fast enough corner, power oversteer is likewise achievable in virtually any car in a slow enough corner. Because torque multiplication from different gear ratios changes power at the wheels, you will often typically have a certain gear where the switch over happens. In a low-powered car, you might only get power oversteer in 1st or 2nd gear, but in a very high-powered one, only the top gears will allow a full throttle corner exit.

This also shows that you have to set your car balance for the most important gears as a car actually has several different effective power levels. You wouldn't want to set up a low powered car so that you are at the edge of oversteer in first gear, because then you would hopelessly understeer in the more often used higher gears.

Before looking at this more in depth, we want to point out that although power oversteer is always accompanied by excessive wheelspin, excessive wheelspin doesn't always cause oversteer. That last sentence might really test your logic skills, but moving on... If a car doesn't have a limited slip differential or it does have one, but it doesn't provide sufficient locking, excessive throttle will just produce inside rear wheelspin. This will severely limit your power put to the ground, but also can be quite hard for a driver to detect. You might not get a significant change in balance if only the inside is spinning and losing traction. If you had more locking in the differential, excessive throttle would cause both rear tires to lose traction from wheelspin and the car would begin to oversteer. So if you have a car that tends to spin the inside rear without going into oversteer, listening for the unnaturally fast rise in engine speed or of course paying attention to the Universal Cue might need to be your guides to detect that wheelspin.

POWER OVERSTEER TIRE FORCES

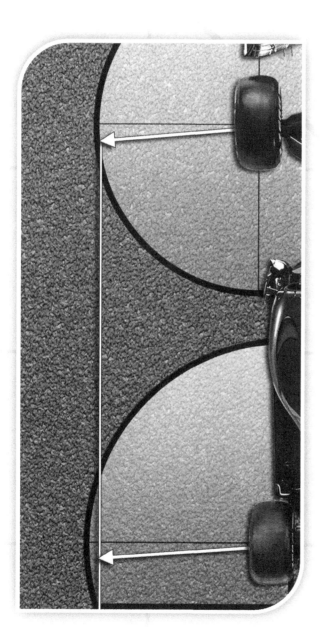

Let's take a look now at what's happening with our tire forces as we go into power oversteer. We will follow the line of force the rear tire makes and compare it to the front. Remember, if the line at the rear is ever closer to the car than the front one is, then the car will begin oversteering and a sensitive driver will be able to detect this oversteer through yaw sensitivity.

This illustration shows a car right at the apex in a slightly understeering state because it needs to have some grip left over at the rear to begin accelerating. Therefore, the line at the rear will not quite be at the edge of the traction circle. You'll probably recognize this as the same state the full-power corner exit car was in at the apex because it's exactly the same at this point.

Partial Throttle

As the driver goes to power, the line moves forward, but right now the driver is not using full power just yet and will still keep it right at the edge of the traction circle. The acceleration made the rear traction circle grow and the front shrink from the load transfer. The circles would steadily change size as more power was applied creating greater acceleration.

This new smaller front circle means that the front tire can produce less lateral force now and so less lateral force is also required of the rear to prevent oversteer. This extra rear tire grip from load transfer is now being used for acceleration and both front and rear tires are right at the limit of grip.

This would actually be the perfect balanced state for a full power throttle exit in a car that had this exact amount of power.

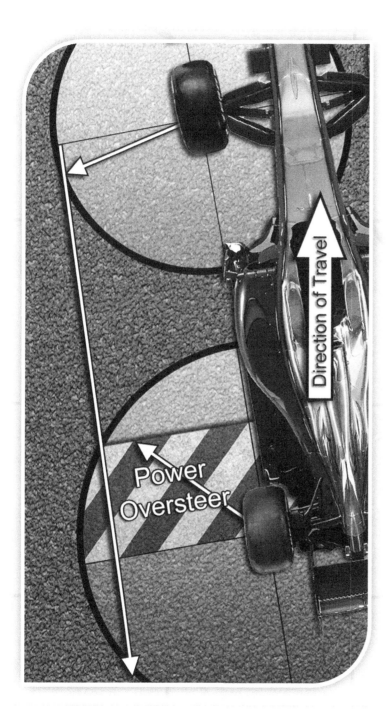

Power Oversteer

Direction of Travel

This car has some extra power though so let's see what happens when we try to keep moving the line forward by applying more throttle.

Remember though, we had already filled up the circle to the point that the edge of the throttle area met the line of force sent back from the front. Any extra power applied won't transfer any more load and change the circle sizes any to allow more throttle. At this point, any more power will force the line inward toward the car reducing lateral force capability for the rear tires as wheelspin increases.

This figures shows how the rear line is now closer to the car than the front, so the car would start to oversteer. From the driver's perspective, they would simply see all this as an increase in throttle while understeering until the car begins to oversteer.

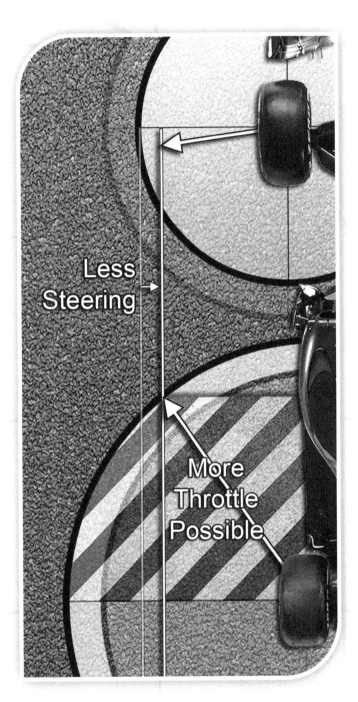

Less Steering

More Throttle Possible

So what is our driver supposed to do with this powerful engine then? Should they increase throttle until the rears reach the edge of the traction circle and then just stay at that limited throttle for the rest of the corner? That's not very fun, is it? Instead, we can use this extra power by reducing steering to match the lateral force required at the rear tires to prevent a spin.

As the driver begins to detect that oversteer, rather than not increasing throttle anymore, they can reduce steering, which brings in the lateral force at the front and thus reduces the lateral grip requirements of the rear tires. This gives them more rear capacity to use for acceleration. This increased acceleration then creates greater rearward load transfer and greater available grip at the rear as the rear circle grows even more.

This can then be used for even more acceleration and so on and so forth. Up to a point of course, this is not an infinite feedback loop that creates unlimited grip.

STEERING VS THROTTLE

So here comes the tricky part. How do you know how much to tradeoff steering and throttle? As usual, we don't ever recommend just doing this as a smooth and arbitrary transition. There has to be a better and more precise way to decide. Well there is and you probably already guessed it. We will again use the Universal Cue. Just like the high-powered front wheel drive car, the only way to truly know how quickly you should trade off steering for throttle is to pay attention to the car's overall movement on track toward the ideal direction.

While in general this will be a steady progression from full steering to full throttle, the ideal rate will depend on the car's lateral vs acceleration potential as well as its power delivery. While a full throttle corner exit will basically give a set arc, if you have excess power you can choose the shape of your acceleration arc just like with the front-wheel drive car. This is what determines where your apex will need to be and therefore ultimately how you do your corner entry.

You have to be careful here because while the general goal is to get to maximum throttle quickly, as with the front-wheel drive car, this might cause someone to use a very late apex and unwind too quickly in an effort to give the rear extra acceleration potential. While this might seem faster because it allows you to increase throttle quicker in the corner, you will be giving up a lot of potential lateral force that you can use. Remember, almost all cars generate more lateral force than propulsive force. They almost never accelerate forward faster than they turn so the latest apex you would generally ever want is going to give you an

> The latest apex you would generally ever want is going to give you an Euler spiral shaped acceleration arc where you would have a fairly linear unwinding of the wheel and just make it to the center steering position at trackout.

Euler spiral shaped acceleration arc where you would have a fairly linear unwinding of the wheel and just make it to the center steering position at trackout. This would typically only be for a very high-powered car though. For more modestly powered cars, you will have a more circular acceleration arc with a slower unwinding through most of the corner exit and then a quicker unwinding closer to the track edge. It's also important to note the difference between unwinding steering and full countersteering. A steering reduction to allow more acceleration potential is beneficial because it keeps the net tire forces pushing you in the ideal direction better. But if you have gotten to the point of so much oversteer that an actual reversal of steering is required, the net tire forces are going in the completely wrong direction and this is definitely considered a mistake.

Remember, our primary goal is to move the car in the ideal direction as best we can and during corner exit, the amount of power we can apply is going to be our greatest limitation for how well we can do that. We almost never have this limitation during corner entry where we are only limited by tire grip, not power. During corner entry, you could think of the brakes as the engine that slows the car down. Brakes can almost always lock up the tires at any speed so in a way you can think of them as an engine with virtually unlimited power to decelerate the tires. So while almost all cars will have a corner entry path in the ideal shape of an Euler spiral, their accelerations arcs during corner exit can vary widely depending on their ability to put power to the ground.

You should also understand that while pressing the brake provides a fairly linear increase in stopping power, the amount of throttle applied doesn't necessarily match the power delivery. For example, depending on your power band, you may only have half the power available at the apex that you have at track out. Because of this, you may start at near full throttle at the apex and then might even have to reduce throttle as the car reaches maximum power at corner exit.

Therefore, it's important to understand that the amount of throttle applied doesn't really matter. What does matter is the actual power delivery to wheels. Sometimes this might require an increase in throttle and sometimes it might require a fairly steady throttle position. The popular driving advice that you should never apply throttle until you are sure you won't have to lift is not always true. Sometimes a partial lift during corner exit is faster if the engine power is increasing rapidly with engine speed. It all depends on the car's power delivery, but the only way to know what is needed is paying attention to your cues.

Luckily though, while the Universal Cue is the final answer to knowing how quickly you should unwind the steering and apply throttle, there are some clues that can help point you in the right direction. Unlike the high power, front-wheel drive car, the powerful rear-wheel drive car does have a shortcut we can go by to see if our corner exit is at least pretty close to optimal. This is not quite as easy as the full-throttle corner exit shortcut, but it does help you as you develop your sensitivity to the Universal Cue. This is also a good way to finish out this book. Understanding why this shortcut works will test your knowledge of many things we have learned so far. Different acceleration arcs, why high-powered cars apex later than slower cars, and how the tire forces are the reason for all this.

So we've now learned that in order to optimize our exit we want the highest combined **vector** acceleration attainable. This means whatever combination of lateral and longitudinal acceleration forces creates the greatest total force. From a driver input standpoint, that means that in a rear wheel drive car we should always be on the limit of oversteer to use the rear tires to the maximum, but also as close to understeer as possible to use the fronts. This is essentially the opposite of the ideal state during corner entry.

From the driver's point of view, this will feel like you are trying to get on the power as **quickly** as possible, but also trying to unwind the steering as **slowly** as possible without causing excessive oversteer. Corner exit should feel like a battle between these two goals. A quicker unwind will allow greater forward acceleration, but only at the cost of the lateral force component and thus the total acceleration force. If the driver unwinds too fast, they will feel this as it being really easy to avoid oversteer even when going hard on the throttle. Sudden increases in power shouldn't be possible. You should have to follow the traction circle around from the side toward the top.

Taking this further, we can deduce that if you have true power oversteer, you normally shouldn't be able to reach full throttle until you are just about going straight at the end of the corner. You can see an example of this by watching a Formula 1 race. The cars will typically either go to full throttle right at the apex if it's a higher gear corner or not until they are just about going straight in a lower gear corner.

> If you can't achieve a full throttle corner exit, you normally shouldn't be able to reach full throttle until you are going straight at the end of the corner.

You can use this shortcut to help determine your apex. If you find yourself able to get to full throttle prior to the end of the corner, you should use an earlier apex. This will force you to have greater total steering needed at corner exit, and therefore unwind slower which puts more lateral load into the tires. You will know you went too far with too early of an apex if you have a good bit of throttle left to apply as you reach the end of the corner. If you can finally just achieve full throttle right as you straighten out the wheel and remove all lateral load you'll know you are on the right track. To understand why this shortcut works, we just have to look at how our acceleration arc is affected by the tire forces.

Corner Exit

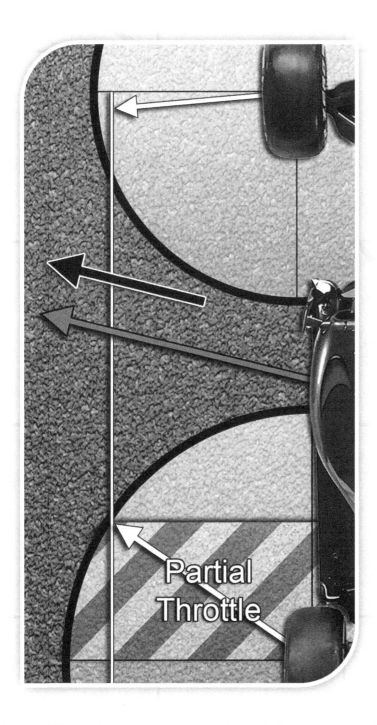

Partial
Throttle

This illustration shows a car that has just passed the apex and went to the maximum throttle possible without excessive oversteer.

To keep the car at the edge of oversteer you can see how the driver has started to relax the steering a little as the line does not quite use all the front tire capacity. The black arrow shows our ideal direction and is pointing down the following straightaway. The long grey line shows the combined tire forces acting on the cars center of gravity. It is ideal right now pointing in exactly the same direction down the track.

If this were full throttle in this car, the driver would carry this state through the rest of the corner. The long grey line would stay at this angle in relation to the car and as the car went through the rest of the corner, it would steadily point in a less optimal direction. This would still be the ideal corner exit for that car however, because it wouldn't have the power

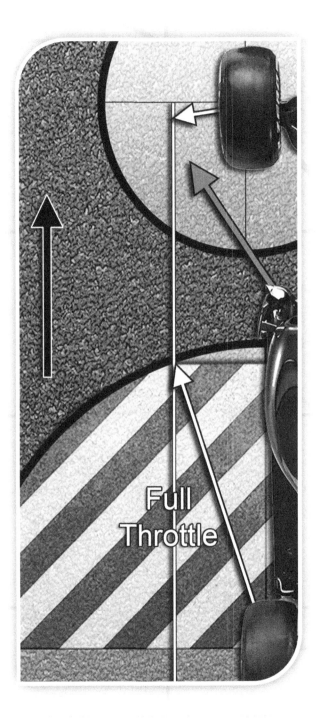

Full
Throttle

to push the tire forces any further forward. This would give us the best total net force during corner exit the car can achieve. This last part is key because if we have more power we can get that line pointed more ideally in the later part of the corner and improve our total net force.

This illustration shows the powerful car now very late in the corner when it has finally achieved full throttle. The combined tire forces are now making the line acting on the center of gravity point very far forward, but notice the line is shorter. The total force is less. The rear tires are at maximum capacity pushing the line as far forward as it can. Note that this rear tire line would be longer than the previous rear tire line because of greater load transfer from the increased acceleration.

To allow the rear tire to provide this forward acceleration however, the front tire cannot send back very much lateral force requirement at all or the car will start to power oversteer. The combined tire force line, although pointed much further forward, will provide less overall force than when the tires were more evenly loaded. Again, almost all cars generate more force while cornering than accelerating. This is also where 4-wheel drive really helps as the force line from the front tire could also be helping push the car forward.

A key point to understand here is that anytime this car goes through a corner it will always progress through these states. The direction of force will always have to go from the side of the car to the front while also shrinking. You cannot skip a degree, so to speak. The only thing the driver can control is the rate at which this happens.

Ideally, the driver will want to keep that force line pointing in the ideal direction with the highest force possible through the corner exit. This explains the battle between steering and throttle. You want to use the maximum combined force possible pushing the car down the track. If the driver apexed too early, there would be greater total steering needed at corner exit. This would require more lateral force requirement sent to the rear tires and would limit the amount of throttle you could use to avoid oversteer. The force line would stay toward the side of the car longer as it turned through the corner and it would start pointing too far toward the inside of the corner. Although the total amount of force would be greater, the amount of that force pushing the car in the ideal direction would be lower than possible.

If on the other hand the driver apexed too late, there would be less steering required through the corner exit and they would be able to get to the state in the second illustration much earlier in the corner exit. Although the force could be directed well, the total amount of force applied throughout the corner exit would be lower than possible. You don't want to get to this state too early because the total amount of force created is less. You want to use those front tires as much as possible throughout the corner exit as well.

Finally reaching full throttle is not ideally achieved right at corner exit because that just happens to be the speed and power level that exactly matches what the tires can provide. The reason is because the driver finally removes all steering and the lateral grip requirement sent back goes away so all of the rear tire capacity can be used for forward acceleration. Very few cars will wheelspin in a straight line at race speeds. If the car does, then this shortcut doesn't work, as you would probably need to delay full throttle until you reached the next gear.

Therefore, this is not a hard rule as it ultimately depends on the car's power delivery. The Universal Cue will always need to be the final answer, but this shortcut can be a useful guide as it's applicable to the vast majority of cars. To recap, if you find yourself able to get to full throttle prior to the end of the corner you should use an earlier apex. This will force you to have greater total steering needed at corner exit, and therefore unwind slower which puts more lateral load into the tires. You will know you have too early of an apex if you have a good bit of throttle left to apply as you reach the end of the corner.

Also again, this doesn't necessarily mean a steady increase in throttle. Throttle position doesn't matter, only power delivery. The power could be climbing rapidly with rpm so the driver might just have the throttle very close to maximum through the entire corner exit or modulating between full and just shy of full while also using as much steering as possible. The point is that if you can't achieve full throttle near the apex, you most likely shouldn't be able to until right at track out.

PERFECT CONTROL

This shortcut as well as every other shortcut we've mentioned is simply a reflection of properly following the Universal Cue. They are just clues that coincide with keeping your forces maximized and heading in the correct direction. They give you breadcrumbs as you improve your skills and sensitivity to the primary cue. Eventually though, they won't be necessary. Once you get to the skill level where the car is the astronaut and the tires are your fire extinguisher, everything else will fall into place. Just maximize and aim your forces correctly. Whatever helps you do that the best is always the correct answer because you will just be following the basic physics at work.

Our goal is not to just have you memorize Line Theory rules or try out different car control techniques to see what works for you. We want you to truly understand why you shouldn't focus on imprecise cues like steering wheel forces or tire noises. We want you to understand why you shouldn't simply try to copy faster drivers or memorize a preplanned set of motions for each corner. Losing is never fun, but losing and not knowing why is worse. We want you to understand why you are slow (or fast!) and how focusing on precise cues like the Universal Cue is the only way to know the right answer, the perfect answer. Naturally gifted drivers are those who drive by these precise cues, these perfect cues, intuitively, often without really understanding them or being able to explain exactly what they are doing. That's why we have spent so much time explaining it for them, because while perfect control may not be intuitive for everyone, it can definitely be learned by just about anyone.

Other Motorsport Education Titles by
PARADIGM SHIFT DRIVER DEVELOPMENT

THE PERFECT CORNER

We will take you through an intuitive and fun lesson in the physics of racing and then we'll apply it as you learn to optimize your driving technique. We will look at real-world racetracks and provide an exact procedure to find the ideal approach all from the driver's eye point of view. Regardless of your current level of driving experience, you can apply these methods today and remove any doubt about what you should be doing on track for good.

THE PERFECT CORNER 2

Ready for the next level? Learn how the physics of racing can be applied to advanced track sections. We show you the rules needed to optimize double apexes, chicanes, and even how the Double Apex Rule can be used to ideally correct mistakes in your line as you drive. The final section will really put you to the test as we break down some of the most complicated corner sequences in the world. You'll see how there is no such thing as a throwaway corner and how every single section of a track can be driven to perfection.

These titles are available wherever quality books are sold or by visiting us at www.paradigmshiftracing.com

Made in the USA
Middletown, DE
17 August 2022

71586156R00077